PROPHETIC INSIGHTS FOR DAILY LIVING

VOLUME 4

~~

Inspired Messages From The Holy Spirit

Sheila Eismann

Books by Sheila Eismann

A STORMY YEAR – BOOK 2 OF THE SABBLONTI SERIES

A WOMAN OF SUBSTANCE – A 12-WEEK BIBLE STUDY

CREATIVE AUTHORS' WORKBOOK JOURNAL – A STEP-BY-STEP GUIDE FOR YOUR WRITING EXPERIENCE – CO- AUTHOR

HEART TO HEART FROM GOD'S WORD

LOVE, THE TIE THAT BINDS – BOOK 3 OF THE SABBLONTI SERIES

JANTZI'S JOKERS – BOOK 1 OF THE SABBLONTI SERIES

POETRY TIME – VOLUME ONE

PROPHETIC INSIGHTS FOR DAILY LIVING – MESSAGES INSPIRED BY THE HOLY SPIRIT – VOLUME 1

PROPHETIC INSIGHTS FOR DAILY LIVING – MESSAGES INSPIRED BY THE HOLY SPIRIT – VOLUME 2

PROPHETIC INSIGHTS FOR DAILY LIVING – MESSAGES INSPIRED BY THE HOLY SPIRIT – VOLUME 3

PROPHETIC INSIGHTS FOR DAILY LIVING – MESSAGES INSPIRED BY THE HOLY SPIRIT – VOLUME 4

RECOGNIZE YOUR CIRCLES

STIRRINGS OF THE SPIRIT

STRAIGHT FROM THE HORSE'S TROUGH

Sheila Eismann

THE CHRISTMAS TIN

Copyright © 2022 by Sheila Eismann.

www.sheilaeismann.com

All rights reserved. No portion of this book may be reproduced, stored in a retrieval system, or transmitted in any form or by any means — electronic, mechanical, photocopy, recording, scanning, or other — except for brief quotations in critical reviews or articles, without the prior written permission of the publisher.

Published by Desert Sage Press
www.desertsagepress.com

Printed and bound in the United States of America.

Cover design by Cathie Richardson. **www.countrygardenstitchery.com**
All rights reserved.

Any trademarks, service marks, product names, or named features are used only for reference, are assumed to be the property of their respective owners, and the use of any one of those terms does not imply an endorsement on the part of the author and/or the publisher.

ISBN: 978-1-7373135-3-3

Library of Congress Control Number: 2022902848

Scriptures are taken from the New King James Version. Copyright 1979, 1980, 1982 by Thomas Nelson, Inc. Used by permission. All rights reserved.

Scripture quotations marked (NIV) are taken from the Holy Bible, New International Version®, NIV®. Copyright © 1973, 1978, 1984, 2011 by Biblica, Inc.® Used by permission of Zondervan. All rights reserved worldwide. www.zondervan.com. The "NIV" and "New International Version" are trademarks registered in the United States Patent and Trademark Office by Biblica, Inc.®

DEDICATION

    This series of workbooks is dedicated to my beloved husband, Dan, who our precious grandkiddos affectionately refer to as "Poppy." He's my best friend, confidant, loyal companion, and fellow believer in our Lord and Savior, Jesus Christ. I will be forever grateful for God knitting our hearts together in His love and giving us compatible and mutually beneficial spiritual giftings.

    We've experienced challenges, supreme blessings, miracles, and victories during the 39 years of our marriage. God has sustained us every single day and step of the way by His mighty right hand, His beloved Son, Jesus Christ, The Holy Spirit, His Word, and His ministering angels.

    We're eternally grateful for all of the divine appointments God has orchestrated with those of His choosing throughout the intersections of our lives.

    It's been the honor and privilege of a lifetime to walk side-by-side with Dan as we continue to learn, laugh, and love together. To God be the glory, both now and forevermore!

ACKNOWLEDGEMENTS

My heartfelt gratitude, sincere appreciation, and blessings are extended to Cathie Richardson, Lesta Chadez, and Marilyn Battisti for their invaluable assistance and encouragement in publishing this set of prophetic workbooks.

It's been a special joy to share this experience with my oldest daughter, Cathie, whose artistic gifts and talents bless me beyond measure. For a real treat, please check out her website: **www.countrygardenstitchery.com**

Fifty-three years ago, Lesta and I lived in the same small rural area. Our paths reconnected at just the right time. Despite navigating her own set of life's challenges, Lesta's dynamic combination of mercy and exhortation is a bonus for any writer. In addition, she's a poet, author, and spiritual songwriter.

Being a retired school teacher, Marilyn operates from a unique vantage point with respect to almost everything she reads and studies, especially as it relates to spiritual matters. I continue to be amazed when reading her thoughts if she opts to post a comment on my website after I've authored one of my blog posts! Since Marilyn has a real heart for intercessory prayer, she's blessed my life immensely as a prayer partner.

In addition, I want to thank my Lord Jesus for helping me every day in every way. With Him, all things are possible. (Matthew 19:26) I'm grateful for The Holy Spirit and His gifts of creativity which are inherent within each of us in various forms.

TABLE OF CONTENTS

Introduction	13
Geese & Godwinks	27
The Wheat, The Harvest & The Mold	35
God's Paintbrush	43
The Multitude of God's Mercies	52
The Mosaic of Your Life	62
Thanksgiving Traditions	71
Your Spiritual Light Assignment	80
A Christmas Blessing	91
Joyful	98
Prophetic Dream – The P.H.S. & The $325	107
Christmas Joy	113
2022 – The Year of Light	119
Our Sustenance Word	127
The One Who Is With Us	138
The Year of God's Rainbow	148
Prophetic Dream – The Book Cover	159
Sign In The Sky	170
Double Bloom – Double Portion	182
No Early Retirement	192
NJD – Don't Quit!	203

About The Author 215

Other Books Available from Sheila and Dan Eismann & Desert Sage Press 217

Notes and Reflections 223

FOREWARD

Woven into the fabric of our lives wherein a silver cord is intertwined throughout the tapestry, there are people in our circle of friends where our hearts are bound together through the Holy Spirit. Sheila Eismann is a special friend that God has placed in my life as the Lord has knit our hearts together in His love. We grew up in the same rural town, and our parents were friends. From this friendship, a bond of love was birthed.

As I have read Sheila's books and followed her writings and blogs over the years, her prophetic visions and dreams have ministered to me in many areas. I give praise to our Lord and Savior Jesus Christ for the many ways He has been with me throughout my life. The Lord especially filled my heart with a living hope through a time of testing when my husband entered into his eternal home in 2019. Special friends like Sheila prayed for me through this difficult journey, and I will be forever grateful for the many ways the Lord has strengthened me and given me hope.

Sheila has a gifting and unique way of weaving in words of wisdom, encouragement, and exhortation as she shares with us what the Lord has given her in visions, dreams, and prophetic words. When we face times of trouble, testing, or tribulation, she has a way of bringing her messages to a practical application in our daily lives by sharing words of comfort and hope while challenging us to pursue a deeper walk with the Lord.

The prophetic visions and dreams the Lord has shared with Sheila are for anyone who wants a fresh infusion of faith and strength to start each day. They are for those walking through difficult seasons of life such as loneliness, grief, or change. The wisdom the Lord shares with her may be for those who are overwhelmed by life's challenges and for those who may be concerned about loved ones or the condition of the world around us. When it seems like the circumstances of life and the storms that surround us are pulling us under, she reminds us that the Lord is the Victor and encourages us to continue to put our trust and hope in Him as He is faithful and true to His promises and His Holy Word.

Every day we need wisdom and fresh insight as we walk out the fullness of our salvation in our journey through this earthly life. The workbooks that Sheila has prepared can be as a devotional and also used in a Bible study. Her prophetic writings will be a blessing to those who have open hearts ready to receive what the Lord has for them.

Lesta Chadez, Poet, Spiritual Song Writer, and Author of *Treasures Hidden In Plain Sight, A Collection of Poems and Short Stories.*

You will be ever so blessed to read the prophetic articles by Sheila Eismann. Each of her visions is a timely message to guide and direct you in your everyday living. Having the inspiration from The Holy Spirit, each of Sheila's writings is a direct appointment for you to individually meet with our Lord Jesus and find manna for your soul. Sheila's prophetic visions will definitely inspire you and lift you to another level of Christianity!

Marilyn Battisti, Retired Educator

INTRODUCTION

Prophetic Insights For Daily Living was written with you, the spiritual seeker, Bible reader, and student, in mind to render assistance regarding spiritual gifts, dreams, visions, and prophetic words.

To introduce this new series of workbooks, I deem it's important to go into greater detail concerning the three revelatory gifts of the Holy Spirit listed in 1 Corinthians 12:4-11. These gifts are the word of wisdom, the word of knowledge, and the discerning of spirits.

"There are diversities of gifts, but the same Spirit. There are differences of ministries, but the same Lord. And there are diversities of activities, but it is the same God who works all in all. But the manifestation of the Spirit is given to each one for the profit *of all:* **for to one is given the word of wisdom through the Spirit, to another the word of knowledge through the same Spirit**, to another faith by the same Spirit, to another gifts of healings by the same Spirit, to another the working of miracles, to another prophecy, **to another discerning of spirits**, to another *different* kinds of tongues, to another the interpretation of tongues. But one and the same Spirit works all these things, distributing to each one individually as He wills." [Emphasis mine]

Writing to the church at Corinth, Paul said, "Now concerning spiritual *gifts*, brethren, I do not want you to be ignorant:" [1 Corinthians 12:1]

During its establishment phase, God did not want the church in Corinth to be ignorant concerning these matters, and His desire is no less for present-day churches or Bible-believing Christians.

An important aspect to remember is the Holy Spirit distributes His gifts to each one individually as He wills. [1 Corinthians 12:11] Every single one of the spiritual gifts outlined in 1 Corinthians 12:4-10 is precisely just that, a gift which cannot be bought, traded, manufactured, contrived, manipulated, or you fill in the blank.

The Holy Spirit gift of the word of wisdom and the gift of the word of knowledge:

"Before we begin our study of the gifts of the Holy Spirit, it is important for us to understand that in the scriptures there is a mingling of gifts, so much so that at times we may question just which gift (or gifts) is being manifested. This need cause us no real concern, for it must be remembered that all of the gifts flow from the same source, The Holy Spirit. If we are unable to identify exactly and classify perfectly, let us not be overly concerned. As humans, it is our nature to draw neat lines of separation and classification, but when we seek to impose this practice upon God, we only frustrate ourselves, and we may generate unnecessary confusion.

The word of wisdom and the word of knowledge are two gifts that often work together. Throughout the Old Testament when the prophets would prophesy, the word of wisdom and the word of knowledge would flow together (knowledge, and what to do about it.) In reading the prophetic books of the Old Testament, you will notice the phrase time and time again, "The WORD of the Lord came to _____ (name)." Examples of this can be found in 1 Kings 17:8; Jeremiah 1:4-8; Ezekiel 1:3; Joel 1:1 and Haggai 1:1.

In the New Testament, much of the writings of Paul, Peter, James, and Jude are the word of wisdom and word of knowledge. Also, John's letters to the churches in Revelation chapters 2-3 are this mixture. The word of wisdom often comes with the word of knowledge so that believers in Christ will know how to apply that knowledge correctly. These gifts are two of the three gifts that 'reveal' something. We call these gifts revelation gifts because they consist of information supernaturally revealed from God. Each of these gifts is the God-given ability to receive from Him facts concerning something, anything, about which it is humanly impossible for us to know, revealed to the believer so that he or she may be protected, pray more effectively, or help someone in need.

The gift of the word of knowledge is supernatural in character. It is not obtained by logic, or deduction, reasoning, etc., or by natural senses, but by supernatural revelation through The Holy Spirit. It is the sheer gift of God. It is not essentially a vocal gift. It is received quietly and inaudibly within the person's spirit. It may become vocal when shared with others.

A basic definition of the word of knowledge: a fragment or small item of God's knowledge, supernaturally revealed to a person by The Holy Spirit.

An example of a spoken word of knowledge can be found in John 1:47-49:

'Jesus saw Nathanael coming toward Him, and said of him, 'Behold, an Israelite indeed, in whom is no deceit!'

Nathanael said to Him, 'How do You know me?'

Jesus answered and said to him, 'Before Philip called you, when you were under the fig tree, I saw you.'

Nathanael answered and said to Him, 'Rabbi, You are the Son of God! You are the King of Israel!'

It is important to consider what the word of knowledge is not:

- It is not human knowledge gained by natural means.

- It is not human knowledge sanctified by God.

- It cannot be gained by intellectual learning, studying books, or pursuing academics.

- It is not the ability to study, understand, or interpret the Bible.

- It is not a psychic phenomenon or extra-sensory perception such as telepathy (the supposed ability to be able to read minds), clairvoyance (the supposed ability to know things that are happening elsewhere), or precognition (the supposed ability to know the future.)

The gifts of the Spirit defy human scientific explanation and are not acquired by ordinary educational processes. No amount of education or learning can produce them. They are not dependent upon innate human qualities. For example, the word of wisdom might be spoken by a person or even less than ordinary wisdom. They are not accentuated natural talents and abilities. The least talented or able may as likely be the agent through whom God works as the most intellectually endowed.

It is a subtle ploy of the great deceiver of our souls to attempt to humanize the supernatural and to reduce the spiritual gifts to the level of mere human endowments, talents, and learned or acquired abilities.

A word of knowledge may be revealed to a believer in any of the following ways:

- A sudden inspiration or a deep inner impression.

- A dream, vision, or picture seen through the eye of the spirit, with the interpretation of what is seen.

- Hearing the voice of God, or of angels, audibly or in the ear of the spirit.

- A living personal word from the Lord through scripture.

- The vocal gifts of the Holy Spirit such as tongues, interpretation of tongues, or prophecy. [1 Corinthians 12:10]

Supernatural visions and dreams are usually the word of wisdom or word of knowledge in operation. Acts 2:17-18 reminds us of what was spoken by the prophet Joel,

> *'And it shall come to pass in the last days, says God,*
> *That I will pour out of My Spirit on all flesh;*
> *Your sons and your daughters shall prophesy,*
> *Your young men shall see visions,*
> *Your old men shall dream dreams.*
> *And on My menservants and on My maidservants*
> *I will pour out My Spirit in those days;*
> *And they shall prophesy.'*

The word of knowledge may not always be fully understood by the receiver or the hearers. It can seem like it's a riddle or a mystery. In the seventh and eighth chapters of the book of Daniel, we read where the prophet was troubled in his spirit, and the visions that were given to him disturbed him greatly. In Daniel 8:27b, God's servant was appalled by the vision, and it was beyond his understanding.

Oftentimes God will use a word of knowledge to uncover sin, bring people to Him, give guidance and direction, minister encouragement, or impart knowledge of future events. Some Bible scholars teach the revelation of future events to be the gift of the word of wisdom rather than the word of knowledge since wisdom usually pertains to what to do in the future.

If you would like to take the time to examine some examples of a word of knowledge in the Bible, I have listed a few from the Old Testament and the New Testament.

Old Testament:

- 1 Samuel 3:10-14

- 1 Samuel 10:17-23

- 1 Kings 19:11-18

- 2 Kings 5:20-27

- 2 Kings 6:8-23

New Testament:

- Luke 2:25-26
- John 1:29-34
- John 6:60-61
- John 13:38
- Acts 5:1-11

Hosea 4:6a reminds us that God's people are destroyed for lack of knowledge. We definitely need the gift of the word of knowledge operating in our lives and churches today!

The word of wisdom is a flash of inspiration. It is a supernatural revelation sufficient for the occasion of the wisdom or purpose of God. It is the wisdom needed to meet a particular situation, answer a particular question, or utilize a particular piece of information.

Once again, it is vital to consider what the word of wisdom is and is not:

- It is not natural wisdom.
- It is not the wisdom gained from academic achievement.
- It is not wisdom gained from experience.
- It is not even the wisdom to understand the Bible.
- It is given as the Holy Spirit wills (1 Corinthians 12:11).
- It is given for a specific need or situation.

A word of wisdom may be revealed to a believer in Christ the same way that I have listed previously for the word of knowledge.

It is helpful to know that we can pray for wisdom, understanding, and knowledge. In Ephesians 1:17, Paul prayed for the spirit of wisdom and revelation. In Colossians 1:9, Paul asked God to fill the believers in the church in Colosse with the knowledge of His will in all wisdom and spiritual understanding.

The following are examples of a word of wisdom found in the Old Testament and the New Testament:

Old Testament:

- Genesis 6:13-21
- Genesis 41:33 with Acts 7:10
- Exodus 28:3; 31:6 and 35:26
- Judges 7:5
- 2 Samuel 5:17-25

New Testament:

- Matthew 2:12-15
- Matthew 21:23-27
- Luke 20:22-26
- John 8:3-7
- Acts 27:23-26[i]

The Holy Spirit gift of discerning of spirits:

"The third gift along with the word of wisdom and word of knowledge that reveals something is the gift of discerning of spirits. It has a narrower range than the other two because it is limited to the spirit world.

Sometimes this gift has been called the gift of discernment which is in error. It is the gift of discerning of spirits. It is not the gift of discerning people; it is the gift of discerning of spirits. There is a huge difference.

From our study of scripture, we learn that there are four basic categories of spirits in the spirit world which are as follows:

- God - John 4:24

- Angels – Hebrews 1:14

- Evil spirits, deceiving spirits and demons - Ephesians 6:12; 1 Timothy 4:1 and Revelation 16:14

- Man - Zechariah 12:1; 1 Corinthians 2:11a

A believer in Christ may be (1) operating under the inspiration of the Holy Spirit; or (2) expressing his or her own thoughts, feelings, and desires from his or her soul or spirit; or (3) allowing an alien spirit to oppress him or her and be bringing thoughts from that wrong spirit. An unbeliever in Christ may be completely possessed by an evil spirit. (Luke 8:26-39) The gift of discerning of spirits immediately reveals what is taking place. This gift is given to know what is in a person and to know the spirit that motivates him or her.

First, we need to define the word 'discern.' It is looking beyond the outward to the inward, literally, 'seeing right through', or 'insight.' In the gift of discerning of spirits, it means to distinguish between good and evil spiritual influences.

The following three verses are a sample of how the word 'discern' is used in the Bible:

- 2 Samuel 14:17 – 'And now your servant [the woman from Tekoa] says, 'May the word of my lord the king bring me rest, for my lord the king is like an angel of God in discerning good and evil. May the LORD your God be with you.' [NIV]

- 2 Samuel 19:35a – 'I [Barzillai the Gileadite] *am* today eighty years old. Can I discern between the good and bad?'

- Ezekiel 44:23 – 'And they [the priests] shall teach My people *the difference* between the holy and the unholy, and cause them to discern between the unclean and the clean.'

Some Biblical scholars believe that if there are no visions, (actually **seeing** the spirit), it is not the gift of discerning of spirits, but rather the gift of the word of knowledge in operation. They reason that if one is informed about a spirit, but has no vision of the spirit, he or she would not **discern** it. In some cases, a WORD comes first, then a vision follows.

Through the gift of discerning of spirits, we can discern the origin of certain actions, teachings, and circumstances that have been inspired by spiritual beings. It is the ability given by God to know what spirit is motivating a person or situation. The gift allows a believer to detect and identify spirits and provides supernatural revelation of the unseen spirit world, both good and evil. The real nature of this gift is knowing and judging – never guessing.

The gift of discerning of spirits is not a natural critical spirit, insight into human nature, human shrewdness, character reading, fault-finding, psychological insight or even spiritual discernment. It is not a spiritual gift to uncover human failings. It is not the spirits of people who have died. It has nothing to do with spiritism or spiritualism. The spirits of departed human beings are not on this earth and to attempt to contact them is forbidden. [Deuteronomy 18:9-12]

Discerning of spirits is needed primarily to reveal the source of spirits. The first and most obvious function of this gift is to reveal the presence of evil spirits in the lives of people or churches. However, it also functions to evaluate the source of a prophetic message, a particular teaching, or some supernatural manifestation. The person functioning with this gift will be able to tell whether the source of the message or act is demonic, divine, or merely human. The gift of discerning of spirits enables a Christian to pick out the source of gifts and messages that truly come from God. Humans cannot be in contact with or understand the spiritual realm except by the power of God or the power of Satan. (1 Corinthians 2:14)

Although the gift has to do primarily with evil spirits, it also is the ability to detect the presence of the Holy Spirit. Visions, seeing Jesus or angels are also included in the discerning of spirits. If one only discerns evil spirits, then the Holy Spirit gift of discerning of spirits is not in operation.

Our natural discernment can be easily fooled. The gift of discerning of spirits is a means of protection from satanic deception. It is easy to confuse the words of the spirit of Satan with those of the Spirit of God. Satan counterfeits the beautiful works of God by creating an outward appearance that is similar to the real work of the Holy Spirit.

Satan is known as the deceiver [Revelation 12:9], the father of lies [John 8:44], and the serpent [Revelation 20:2]. All these titles signify the subtle, crafty deceptiveness which he uses to bring about evil whenever he can. Many times, his counterfeit is so plausible that one will be entirely deceived unless someone is present who functions with the supernatural gift of discerning of spirits. If demon activity was always so obviously reeking with evil and wicked intent, as we tend to imagine, there would no use for this gift of the Holy Spirit."[ii]

The following are examples of discerning of spirits found in the Old Testament and the New Testament:

Old Testament:

- Genesis 21:17-19

- Leviticus 19:31
- Deuteronomy 32:17
- Judges 13:3-7
- 1 Samuel 16:14-15, 23
- 1 Samuel 28:11-19
- 1 Kings 19:5-8
- 2 Kings 6:17
- 2 Chronicles 18:18-22
- Zechariah 3:1-2

New Testament:
- Matthew 1:20-21
- Matthew 16:23
- Luke 1:11-20; 26-38
- Luke 13:11, 16
- Acts 12:7-10
- Acts 13:9-11
- Acts 27:23-24
- 1 John 4:1"

Despite teachings to the contrary, God's people do receive dreams, visions, and prophetic words today. Here's a basic overview of this aspect of the revelatory realm:

1. God communicates through His prophets in one of two ways. "Let the prophet who has a dream tell the dream, but let him who has my word speak my word faithfully."[iii] As an aside, why would God want to stop communicating to us through prophets? Has He stopped speaking? Do people no longer need to hear from Him?

2. *Nābiy'* prophet. One of the ways God communicates to us is through a *nābiy'* prophet. "This word describes one who was raised up by God and, as such, could only proclaim that which the Lord gave him to say. A prophet could not contradict the Law of the Lord or speak from his own mind or heart."[iv] "I [God] will raise up for them a prophet [*nābiy'*] like you [Moses] from among their brothers. And I will put my words in his mouth, and he shall speak to them all that I command him."[v] Jeremiah was a *nābiy'* prophet, and he tried to refrain from giving the word of the Lord because doing so made him "a reproach and derision all day long."[vi] However, he could not refrain from giving the word of God.

> If I say, "I will not mention him,
>   or speak any more in his name,"
> there is in my heart as it were a burning fire
>   shut up in my bones,
> and I am weary with holding it in,
>   and I cannot.[vii]

3. *Hōzeh* prophets. Another way that God communicates to us is through a *hōzeh* or *chōzeh* prophet (hereinafter *hōzeh* prophet). "The word is "[a] masculine noun meaning a seer, prophet. . . . The word means one who sees or perceives; it is used in parallel with the participle of the verb that means literally to see, to perceive. . . . It appears that the participles of *hōzeh* and *rā'āh* function synonymously. But, terminology aside, a seer functioned the same as a prophet, who was moved by God and had divinely given insight."[viii] *Rā'āh* or *rō'eh* is "a verb meaning to see" and can "connote a spiritual observation and comprehension by means of seeing visions."[ix]

A prophet can function as both a *nābiy'* prophet and a *hōzeh* prophet. For example, Jeremiah functioned as both.

But the Lord said to me,
> "Do not say, 'I am only a youth';
> for to all to whom I send you, you shall go,
> and whatever I command you, you shall speak.
>   . . . .
>   declares the Lord."

Then the Lord put forth His hand and touched my mouth, and the Lord said to me:
> "Behold, I have put My words in your mouth.
>   . . . .
> And the word of the Lord came to me, saying, "Jeremiah, what do you see?" And I said, "I see an almond branch." Then the Lord said to

me, "You have seen well, for I am watching over my word to perform it."[x]

King David was assigned all three types of prophets.

Now the acts of King David, from first to last, are written in the Chronicles of Samuel the seer [rā'āh], and in the Chronicles of Nathan the prophet [nāḇiy'], and in the Chronicles of Gad the seer [hōzeh], with accounts of all his rule and his might and of the circumstances that came upon him and upon Israel and upon all the kingdoms of the countries.[xi]

4. **Examples of the ministry of prophets include the following:**

  a. **Rebuking someone for sin.**

  The LORD sent Nathan the prophet to David to tell him a story about a rich man who stole and prepared for eating a lamb that had been raised in the home of a poor man.[xii]

  Then David's anger was greatly kindled against the man, and he said to Nathan, "As the LORD lives, the man who has done this deserves to die, and he shall restore the lamb fourfold, because he did this thing, and because he had no pity."[xiii]

  Nathan then said to David "You are the man!" referring to David having Uriah the Hittite killed in battle in order to cover the sin of David's adultery with Bathsheba.[xiv]

  b. **Turning peoples' hearts to the LORD.**

  An angel appeared to Zechariah and told him that Elizabeth, his wife who was barren and advanced in years, would have a child, "[a]nd he [John the Baptist] will turn many of the children of Israel to the Lord their God."[xv]

  c. **Bringing people back into a covenant relationship with God.**

  And they abandoned the house of the LORD, the God of their fathers, and served the Asherim and the idols. And wrath came upon Judah and Jerusalem for this guilt of theirs. Yet he sent prophets among them to bring them back to the LORD. These testified against them, but they would not pay attention.[xvi]

  d. **Warning of what will occur in the future.**

  Now in these days prophets came down from Jerusalem to Antioch. And one of them named Agabus stood up and foretold by the Spirit that there would be a great famine over all the world (this took place in the days of Claudius). So the disciples determined, everyone according to his ability, to send relief to the brothers living in Judea. And they did so, sending it to the elders by the hand of Barnabas and Saul.[xvii]

e. Exhorting and strengthening the brethren.

And Judas and Silas, who were themselves prophets, encouraged and strengthened the brothers with many words.[xviii]

f. Giving divine direction.

Now there were in the church at Antioch prophets and teachers, Barnabas, Simeon who was called Niger, Lucius of Cyrene, Manaen a lifelong friend of Herod the tetrarch, and Saul. While they were worshiping the Lord and fasting, the Holy Spirit said, "Set apart for me Barnabas and Saul for the work to which I have called them." Then after fasting and praying they laid their hands on them and sent them off.[xix]

g. Speaking against sin; warning of judgment, and preaching about hope and renewal.

Then the LORD put out his hand and touched my mouth. And the LORD said to me,
> "Behold, I have put my words in your mouth.
> See, I have set you this day over nations and over kingdoms,
> to pluck up and to break down,
> to destroy and to overthrow,
> to build and to plant."[xx]

Jeremiah's message is threefold: (1) he must **pluck up** and **break down**, which refers to preaching against sin; (2) he must **destroy** and **overthrow**, which relates to messages concerning judgment; and (3) he must **build** and **plant**, which means he must preach about hope and renewal."[xxi]

All prophets do not have the same anointing or spiritual assignments. Some are called to prophesy to the people, some to persons in government, some to individuals, and some to geographic regions, mountains, land, rivers, etc. In addition, some receive prophecies more frequently than others. "Do not despise prophecies, but test everything; hold fast what is good."[xxii]

We are not to blindly accept what is prophesied. In church, "[l]et two or three prophets speak and let the others weigh what is said. If a revelation is made to another sitting there, let the first be silent. For you can all prophesy one by one, so that all may learn and all be encouraged, and the spirits of prophets are subject to prophets."[xxiii] A prophet may be male or female.[xxiv]

My personal prayer is that you will be enlightened, strengthened, and encouraged as you study this workbook and record what God, Jesus, and The Holy Spirit reveal to you. Time spent with Them along with reading and studying the Bible yields great dividends.

Please check out my new website: **www.sheilaeismann.com**

Also, if you would like to send an email or have questions about this workbook, my address is **sheila@sheilaeismann.com**. Thank you!

"The LORD bless you and keep you;
The LORD make His face shine upon you,
And be gracious to you;
The LORD lift up His countenance upon you,
And give you peace." (Numbers 6:24-26)

Geese & Godwinks

October 20, 2021

Encouragement

Geese & Godwinks may sound like a strange combination for this week's prophetic blog post. When a flock of ten geese flew directly over my head earlier today on my morning prayer walk, I knew God was communicating directly to me via one of His Godwinks. I like to think of them as being heaven's gifts sent special delivery just to me!

It took me a while to put this together as I deemed geese would just randomly appear overhead just any old time they desired. Typically, geese fly south ahead of the winter months, but they're heaven sent year-round in my neck of the woods.

The uncanny thing is the geese not only bless us with their flyovers, but they honk loudly when doing so just as if to say, "Howdy! How are you doing today?" There have been times when they've been flying closely overhead and will suddenly circle back around, so they can fly directly over us. They appear when I need an extra dose of encouragement or wisdom. Obviously, the geese don't know this, but God in heaven surely does because He's omniscient.

The verse that comes to me is, "Are not two sparrows sold for a copper coin? And not one of them falls to the ground apart from your Father's will. But the very hairs of your head are all numbered. Do not fear therefore; you are of more value than many sparrows." (Matthew 10:29-31)

These verses ultimately gave birth to the popular Christian song, "His eye is on the sparrow" which has been sung by various artists throughout the years. Listening to the verses can envelop us in God's comfort, care, and assurance.

Teamwork makes the dream work!

One of our grandson's favorite sayings is, "Teamwork makes the dream work!" TJ loves every aspect of football. This year he played for the Wolfpack. While not participating at the university level with a team boasting that name, TJ learned a lot and is as enthusiastic as ever moving forward.

Prophetic symbols for geese are loyalty, **teamwork**, and family. As they fly, they're laser-focused upon companionship and friendship. They'll defend and stand by others of their flock until they die. Everyone should be so blessed as to have enduring, faithful friends such as these.

Additional symbols for geese are courage and fearlessness. After all, they've been known to fly through blinding snow to get to their destination.

Let your dreams take flight.

From a literary standpoint, wild geese represent a sense of community, care, and compassion. They fly together in a flock, but there have been times that I've seen a lone goose flying overhead honking to beat the band. This would symbolize pursuing an individual path in life. Another message could be that it's high time for you to take flight, begin a journey, and pursue your dreams. Let your dreams take flight!

Just for geese grins, check out this weblink for goose symbolism:

https://symbolismandmetaphor.com/goose-symbolism/

Godwinks are gifts.

Movies, poems, blogs, and books have all been written and produced regarding the subject of Godwinks.

Just what is a Godwink, anyway?

"**God wink** *n.* something taken as evidence that a higher power is at work; a coincidence. **Editorial Note**: The term was popularized by Squire Rushnell in his 2003 book When God Winks and in his subsequent books. (source: Double-Tongued Dictionary)"

"**An event or personal experience**, often identified as coincidence, so astonishing that it is seen as a sign of divine intervention, especially when perceived as the answer to a prayer. noun. 113. 8. Alternative form of God wink."

I like to think of Godwinks as heaven's gifts via special delivery from God Himself. He has uniquely created each of us and knows precisely what we need and when we need it. Ergo, there will be times when He delivers it via a Godwink!

If the supernatural realm is something you desire to learn more about, I would encourage you to continue reading your Bible and paying close attention to the dreams, visions, and visitations explained in Scripture. You might also enjoy reading my blog post from last week focusing upon the supernatural: https://sheilaeismann.com/heaven-sent/

She sees threes.

One of my dear friends and fellow authors sees a lot of threes during her travels and in everyday life. I felt prompted to remind her to watch for threes on a recent trip to visit her family. During the course of several days, she emailed and texted me describing various encounters with the number three. This is one of the unique ways God chooses to speak to her, and they are God's special Godwinks just for her.

The number three is symbolic of many things, some of which are: the Trinity; the counsel of God; complete; perfect; divine fullness; a time frame such as 3 days, 3 months, or 3 years; resurrection (Jesus was resurrected on the third day – 1 Corinthians 15:4); The Holy Spirit; witness; spirit, soul, and body; and the third heaven.

Prophetic Insights For Daily Living.

#1. Have you been the recipient of Godwinks in the past? If so, in what form did they appear, and how did this minister to you?

_____
_____
_____
_____

#2. The fun aspect of Godwinks is tying the symbolism to the way that God speaks to you. I've memorized the various aspects represented by geese, so when I see them flying directly overhead and honking wildly, I just grin as widely as I can. This makes my heart and spirit so happy!

#3. If you've not experienced anything like this, pray and ask God to begin to surprise you just when you least expect it. While you're at it, pray for others you know who would enjoy a similar experience.

#4. Have you been waiting for one of your dreams to take flight? If so, now may just be the time. Pray and ask God to send you a confirmation via one of His Godwinks.

So, dear friends and fellow readers, while it might not be sparrows flying overhead, it's geese, and I know God is watching over me. May He do the same for you!

Sheila Eismann, Prophetic Seer, Blogger, Author, & Teacher, publishes her weekly blog posts endeavoring to encourage others through God's word. Her writings include teaching and instructions on how to apply prophetic insights for daily living.

Please subscribe to receive new blog posts on her website at www.sheilaeismann.com. by clicking the "Subscribe" button in the far upper right-hand corner of her Home webpage.

(Please feel free to use this page to sketch your "Godwink" or to paste a photo or picture here to help remind you of how God is watching over you!)

The Wheat, The Harvest, & The Mold

October 28, 2021

Prophetic Words

The recent, long-awaited rains might have delayed the last planting of winter wheat in our region that ranks 7th in the nation for the production of this vital food. Pyramid-shaped piles of sugar beets gracing our landscape signal their harvest is in full swing. Our first frost has flattened the green vines causing the pumpkins to pop like bright orange polka dots in patches.

When worshipping the Lord, I heard, "I'm removing you from the old mold." Mama's well-used, aluminum kitchen mold that she used for Jello® recipes flashed through my mind. Thankfully, none of our family was fond of that ghastly green-colored kind. All of us favored red flavors with sliced bananas placed inside before a complete jelling. I'm just kidding – if you prefer green Jello, enjoy! Let's connect this life cycle of the wheat, the harvest, and the mold, shall we?

The purpose of winter wheat.

Winter wheat is planted to decrease erosion from runoff of water and wind and to improve soil aeration. It helps to stabilize the soil, reduce the number of weeds and plant diseases, and control insect infestation. Recovery of soil fertility is another benefit.

The key thing with winter wheat is that it requires either very cold or freezing temperatures for extended periods of time to launch the reproductive stage. So, if it does not go through this process and endure the cold, it will not produce seed.

https://www.cropprophet.com/winter-wheat-production-by-state-top-11/

Green Fields & White Fields

The image in this week's prophetic blog post features a healthy field of green winter wheat. The most important fields are mentioned in John 4:34-38, "Jesus said to them, "My food is to do the will of Him who sent Me, and to finish His work. Do you not say, 'There are still four months and *then* comes the harvest'? Behold, I say to you, lift up your eyes and look at the fields, for they are already white for harvest! And he who reaps receives wages, and gathers fruit for eternal life, that both he who sows and he who reaps may rejoice together. For in this the saying is true: 'One sows and another reaps.' I sent you to reap that for which you have not labored; others have labored, and you have entered into their labors."

The four months referred to in the above passage pertains to the barley planting and harvesting cycle. The Israelites' harvest began at Passover which is in the spring of the year.

In metaphorical language, Jesus is encouraging His disciples to literally look at the agricultural and spiritual harvest fields right before their very eyes. This passage of scripture mentioned in the 4th chapter of the gospel of John occurred after Jesus encountered the Samaritan woman at the well. She literally could be considered the first evangelist in the Bible as she returned to her village and told them of the Savior of the world. Many returned to meet Jesus and ultimately believed in Him. (John 4:39-42)

After Jesus selected His 12 apostles, He also appointed seventy others with the following instructions, "Then He said to them, 'The harvest truly *is* great, but the laborers *are* few; therefore pray the Lord of the harvest to send out laborers into His harvest.'" (Luke 10:1-2)

Harvest appears in approximately 80 different places in scripture. My favorite spot is God's promise in Genesis 8:22, "While the earth remains, seedtime and harvest, cold and heat, winter and summer, and day and night, shall not cease."

Not that kind of mold!

When I heard in my spirit, "I'm removing you from the old mold," I knew which kind of noun form of *mold* the Lord was referring to. It's (a) below as opposed to (b).

(a) "a distinctive and typical style, form, or character."

(b) "a superficial often woolly growth produced especially on damp or decaying organic matter or living organisms by a fungus (as of the order Mucorales); a fungus that produces mold."

By inference, if the old mold we've poured ourselves into, even without realizing it, isn't producing a harvest, God desires to remove it for the sake of His kingdom. He will be doing something new in our lives with the overarching purpose of planting and harvesting. The number 8 is connected with new beginnings.

https://sheilaeismann.com/exercise-your-faith/

Supernatural Yellow Hope Flower

This is the 8th petal on the supernatural, yellow, hope flower which is connected to the number 8 = new beginnings. God is removing you from the old mold and assigning something new to you that's connected to the harvest.

Everything Has It's Appointed Time.

According to Ecclesiastes 3:2b, there is

"A time to plant,
And a time to pluck *what is* planted;"

One spiritual application of this verse is when God planted Israel as a nation in the land of Canaan in the Old Testament, He plucked it up and sent it into exile twice, and replanted it after the Israelites' Babylonian captivity. The books of Ezra and Nehemiah are good ones to study if you are interested in this. Following Jesus' death, crucifixion, ascension into heaven, and the diaspora of the early Christians, it was almost two millennia before Israel was replanted as a nation in May of 1948.

Joanna

The name *Joanna* was quickened unto me which means God is gracious. Who knows, you just might encounter a woman named Joanna in your new field!

A field symbolizes the church universal or a particular church, a believer in Christ, the world, or harvest (someone in the field.)

Prophetic Insights For Daily Living:

#1. Just like the winter wheat must endure temperature extremes in order to produce a seed, there are times in our Christian walk when we will feel like we've been left out in the cold by others or through trials and tribulations, but God will never leave us nor forsake us. (Joshua 1:9 and Hebrews 13:5-6)

#2. Is Jesus calling you as a laborer into a new harvest field? If so, where is it? What is your new beginning? Watch for signposts and confirmations.

_____
_____
_____

#3. It can be most unsettling to have our life cycle interrupted, but God's plans stand firm in the heavens. May we be flexible and cooperate with Him.

#4. Just like there are fields ripe for harvest in our valley right now, there are multitudes among us ready to receive the good news of the gospel of Jesus Christ, so their names can remain in the Lamb's Book of Life. (Revelation 3:5)

#5. There's a gentle urging to evaluate our lives to see if there are areas that have grown fruitless and need to be plucked up. (Ecclesiastes 3:2b) God will be faithful to show us as we spend time in His word and prayer with Him. He is gracious (the meaning of the name Joanna). Wouldn't it be amazing if you met someone named Joanna in your new field assignment and life cycle? Whoa, God!

_____

_____

_____

_____

Here's a little acrostic poem I authored a few years ago titled ~~

HARVEST

Help me to see the lost,

As I travel through this day.

Ready my heart to help,

Various people are still at bay.

Everyone can use a helping hand,

Some will choose Your way.

Tomorrow may be too late!

In God's kingdom, it's harvest time every day!

Sheila Eismann, Prophetic Seer, Blogger, Author & Teacher, publishes her weekly blog posts endeavoring to encourage others through God's word. Her writings include teaching and instructions on how to apply prophetic insights for daily living. Please subscribe to receive new blog posts on her website at www.sheilaeismann.com. by clicking the "Subscribe" button in the far upper right-hand corner of her Home webpage.

God's Paintbrush

November 3, 2021

Inspiration

The gorgeous, glorious blends delivered through God's sunrises and sunsets rival even the most cherished paintings of our favorite artist. The above image captured on my phone a few mornings ago doesn't do the original picture it's due justice and majesty. When I embarked upon my early walk, I marveled at the breathtaking creation and color combination designed by our Creator. I've chosen to call this picture, "God's Paintbrush" via His sunrise.

Bright orange hues ascended above the treetops like an airplane heading upward to 30,000 feet high in the sky. The display of blue and orange colors accentuating the clouds reminded me of an artist holding his palette in his left hand as he mixed the colors before painting.

The color orange symbolizes glory and wisdom. Since I've been praying for more wisdom of late, I deem this was one way in which God is answering my prayers. It's a treasure hunt to watch for signs in the heavens.

Blue represents the color of heaven. Light blue is symbolic of the human spirit. When we focus upon the color blue, it's a reminder from Matthew 6:33, "But seek first the kingdom of God and His righteousness, and all these things shall be added to you."

Sometimes in our flesh, we don't want to seek first the kingdom of God and His righteousness. The battle between the flesh and our spirit will continue as long as we live in our earthly bodies. (Galatians 5:16-26)

Viewing the striations of the orange and blue mix in this photo, it's as if God is infusing the human spirit (light blue) with His glory and wisdom (orange).

In studying the image accompanying this week's prophetic blog post, I've not been able to arrive at any conclusion. Do you see any pictures or images or how does this photo speak to you?

Studying cloud formations can be fun and spiritually insightful. I authored a recent blog post titled *Supernatural Sights & Sounds* wherein I posed the question of discerning pictures in the clouds.

https://sheilaeismann.com/heaven-sent/

Supernatural Sights & Sounds

Our great state is the recipient of majestic sunrises and sunsets which delight our eyes and souls. While this particular sunrise is more orange than red, this little ditty flitted through my mind,

"Red sky at night, sailors' delight.

Red sky at morning, sailors take warning."

The following is an abbreviated history regarding this saying.

"The rhyme is a rule of thumb used for weather forecasting during the past two millennia. It is based on the reddish glow of the morning or evening sky, caused by trapped particles scattering the blue light from the sun in a stable air mass.

"If the morning skies are of an orange-red glow, it signifies a high-pressure air mass with stable air-trapping particles, like dust, which scatters the sun's blue light. This high pressure is moving towards the east, and a low-pressure system moves in from the west. Conversely, in order to see 'red sky' in the evening, high-pressure air mass from the west scatters the blue light in the atmospheric particles, leaving the orange-red glow. High-pressure air mass signifies stable weather, while low pressure signifies unstable weather.

"Because of different prevailing wind patterns around the globe, the traditional rhyme is generally not correct at lower latitudes of both hemispheres, where prevailing winds are from east to west. The rhyme is generally correct at middle latitudes where, due to the rotation of the Earth, prevailing winds travel west to east."

https://en.wikipedia.org/wiki/Red_sky_at_morning

Is your geographic region located at "middle latitudes which are a spatial region on Earth located between the latitudes 23°26'22" and 66°33'39" north, and 23°26'22" and 66°33'39" south? It's the latitudes of the temperate zones or from about 30 to 60 degrees north or south of the equator."

_____

_____

_____

_____

A Challenge From Scripture.

During His earthly ministry, Jesus had many naysayers, scoffers, and challengers. Chief among these were the Pharisees, Sadducees, and scribes. At Matthew 16:1-4, the Pharisees and Sadducees sought a sign from Jesus.

"Then the Pharisees and Sadducees came, and testing Him asked that He would show them a sign from heaven. He answered and said to them, 'When it is evening you say, '*It will be* fair weather, for the sky is red'; and in the morning, '*It will be* foul weather today, for the sky is red and threatening.' Hypocrites! You know how to discern the face of the sky, but you cannot *discern* the signs of the times. A wicked and adulterous generation seeks after a sign, and no sign shall be given to it except the sign of the prophet Jonah.' And He left them and departed."

While this passage of scripture was poignantly directed at a specific audience during New Testament times, it's incumbent upon us to readily discern the signs of the times in which we're living as the landscape is dramatically changing daily on every front. We need Godly wisdom to navigate every sphere of our lives. I harken back to one of the prophetic symbolisms for the color orange which is wisdom. If we lack wisdom in any area of our lives, God is patiently waiting for us to ask Him for it.

"If any of you lacks wisdom, let him ask of God, who gives to all liberally and without reproach, and it will be given to him. But let him ask in faith, with no doubting, for he who doubts is like a wave of the sea driven and tossed by the wind. For let not that man suppose that he will receive anything from the Lord; *he is* a double-minded man, unstable in all his ways." (James 1:5-8)

The Correct Kind of Wisdom.

"Who *is* wise and understanding among you? Let him show by good conduct *that* his works *are done* in the meekness of wisdom. But if you have bitter envy and self-seeking in your hearts, do not boast and lie against the truth. This wisdom does not descend from above, but *is* earthly, sensual, demonic. For where envy and self-seeking *exist,* confusion and every evil thing *are* there. But the wisdom that is from above is first pure, then peaceable, gentle, willing to yield, full of mercy and good fruits, without partiality and without hypocrisy. Now the fruit of righteousness is sown in peace by those who make peace." (James 3:13-18)

Prophetic Insights For Daily Living.

#1. Are you an artist in real life? If so, what's your favorite medium such as oil painting, sketching, pen and ink drawing, etc.?

#2. Who is your favorite artist and why? My husband and I especially enjoy paintings of western landscapes. Fred Choate, a very talented local artist, painted the Idaho side of the Jarbidge Mountain Range. This painting showcases a herd of wild horses grazing on the top of a ridge overlooking a deep, volcanic rock crevice. Sagebrush is sprinkled throughout the landscape. The snow-capped mountain peaks form the perfect border and backdrop for this prized work. It's one of those pictures you could sit and look at for hours as it speaks of the various elements of nature and creation at its finest and in its peaceful state.

#3. As we continue to yield to God, Jesus, and The Holy Spirit, our spiritual portraits are being painted by God's paintbrush. What does yours look like? If you don't quite know, pray and ask God to show you. I'm sure that He would be delighted to do so.

#4. Do you need help or wisdom discerning the signs of the times in which we are living? Time spent in prayer and reading God's word are guaranteed assistance. Prophetic journaling is a wonderful exercise to accompany your quiet time with Jesus.

#5. If you're not accustomed to viewing sunrises and sunsets, I would encourage you to start doing so. God created the heavens and the earth. He named each star if you can imagine that. (Isaiah 40:26) The sunrise, sunset, and myriads of skyscapes have been the inspiration for plenty of stories, songs, conversations, and paintings. Keep looking up, and prepare to be amazed!

"The heavens declare the glory of God; the skies proclaim the work of his hands." (Psalm 19:1 – NIV)

Sheila Eismann, Prophetic Seer, Blogger, Author & Teacher, publishes her weekly blog posts endeavoring to encourage others through God's word. Her

writings include teaching and instructions on how to apply prophetic insights for daily living.

Please subscribe to receive new blog posts on her website at www.sheilaeismann.com. by clicking the "Subscribe" button in the far upper right-hand corner of her Home webpage.

The Multitude of God's Mercies

November 9, 2021

Holidays

As the Thanksgiving season approaches, the Psalmist reminds us, "Oh, give thanks to the LORD, for He is good! For his mercy *endures* forever." (Psalm 106:1) Thankfully, forever is a very long time, so we can still be the recipients of such a magnificent gift from God. Continuing to read through this psalm, we are reminded that the Israelites traversing in Egypt in approximately 1440 B.C. did not remember the multitude of God's mercies. (Verse 7b) Despite this, Psalm 106:45 declares that for Israel's sake, God remembered His covenant with them, and relented according to the multitude of His mercies. In this week's prophetic blog post, let's take a look at both the give and receive aspects of mercy.

Today, November 8, 2021, marks the 30th anniversary of our daughter's tragic automobile accident in which she miraculously survived. For our family, this is a "Red Letter Day" as we remember the multitude of God's mercies which He poured out on us through a turbulent journey until Christi's health was restored. I kept a prophetic journal of this epoch battle to record how God helped us and brought her back from the brink of death. Later, I authored a book titled *Stirrings of The Spirit* wherein I recount the multitude of God's mercies and His miraculous intervention time after time.

https://sheilaeismann.com/product/spiritual-growth/

The Hebrew word for mercy is *hesed* which is Strong's H2617. It means goodness, kindness, lovingkindness, and faithfulness.

https://www.blueletterbible.org/lexicon/h2617/kjv/wlc/0-1/

I've heard mercy defined as God's grace, i.e., unmerited favor, bestowed upon us.

Serving God With The Spiritual Gift of Mercy

At Romans 12:3-8, the Apostle Paul teaches us about God-given abilities that are to be used to edify and encourage fellow believers in Christ.

In this passage of scripture, there are seven gifts listed:

Perceiver (Prophecy)

Server (Ministry)

Teacher

Exhorter

Giver

Administrator (Leader)

Compassionate (Merciful) Person

It's interesting that Romans 12:8 states, "he who shows mercy, with cheerfulness."

There were so many medical personnel who assisted with Christi's recovery for which we will be forever thankful. Some of the nurses exuded mercy like nothing I've ever witnessed. I concluded afterward that perhaps people given the mercy gifting gravitate to the nursing field. People especially need a lot of mercy when they are injured and hurting. Their family members do likewise.

Everything that needed to be done for us, from the date of Christi's accident until she walked out of the hospital 63 days later, was taken care of by our family, church family, friends, and neighbors. Some of you reading this week's prophetic blog post are included in the above-listed people for which we are eternally grateful.

Beyond Lip Service

There's an even greater gauntlet thrown down in the New Testament regarding the subject of mercy.

In the second chapter of James, the Apostle James is warning the church at Jerusalem against personal favoritism, especially as it relates to different treatments for the rich versus the poor. James 2:13 cautions, "For judgment is without mercy to the one who has shown no mercy. Mercy triumphs over judgment."

The Greek word for mercy in verse 13 is *eleos* which is Strong's 1656, and it means "mercy: kindness or goodwill towards the miserable and the afflicted, joined with a desire to help them."

https://www.blueletterbible.org/lexicon/g1656/kjv/tr/0-1/

The obvious challenge and instruction are that it's hardly sufficient to just express merciful sentiments when someone is experiencing tragedy or hardship. There must be a plan to help in any tangible way possible which stems from a genuine, heartfelt desire that will put actions and steps to merciful words.

WDJD – What Does Jesus Desire?

Jesus, The Savior of the world Who gave His life for all mankind, strongly rebuked the Pharisees who had challenged His disciples on a particular occasion.

For a bit of history, I love that Jesus called Matthew, a tax collector who was considered a traitor by the Jews, as one of His twelve disciples. Tax collectors were typically despised because some of them collected more taxes than necessary, which overflow found its way into the collectors' collective pockets, highly enriching themselves.

After Jesus had called Matthew to be one of his disciples, he sat down with his fellow tax collectors, sinners, Jesus, and His disciples. When the Pharisees saw this, they lit into the disciples, "Why does your Teacher eat with tax collectors and sinners?"

"When Jesus heard *that,* He said to them, 'Those who are well have no need of a physician, but those who are sick. But go and learn what *this* means: '*I desire mercy and not sacrifice.*' For I did not come to call the righteous, but sinners, to repentance." (Matthew 9:11-13)

When He said, "I desire mercy and not sacrifice," Jesus was quoting the Old Testament prophet, Hosea, in this verse. (Hosea 6:6)

The irony here is that Jesus refers to the Pharisees as righteous; however, that is only how they perceived themselves. God had previously judged their sacrifices without mercy as entirely worthless. God is far more interested in a person's actions toward the hurting and those in need than external rituals and lip service.

In December 2020, I authored a blog post titled, "The Frozen Footprint." I challenged my reading audience at the time, "Are you willing to sacrifice the comforts of warmth (people were outside in the frigid cold searching with lanterns in the prophetic vision), your time and plans to help someone enter the kingdom of heaven before it's too late?" This would literally be putting footsteps of action to merciful words!

https://sheilaeismann.com/seek-the-lost/

Prophetic Insights For Daily Living

#1. Do you know what your spiritual giftings are? If not, here's a book that I highly recommend titled *Discover Your God-Given Gifts* by Don and Katie Fortune. As you work your way through the book, there are self-administered tests and compilation profile sheets to help you discover or affirm your gifts.

_____
_____
_____
_____
_____

https://www.amazon.com/s?k=discover+your+god+given+gifts+by+don+%26+katie+fortune&crid=XZMM2MECF6J6&sprefix=discover+your+God%2Caps%2C279&ref=nb_sb_ss_ts-doa-p_3_17

#2. Has there been a time in your life when others have exercised their mercy and put actions to their words? If so, how did this minister to you?

_____
_____
_____
_____
_____

#3. Would you like to be a more merciful person? A topical, Biblical study on the subject of mercy is so beneficial as this allows us to view mercy through God's eyes.

_____
_____
_____
_____
_____

#4. During Thanksgiving, make a list of the things for which you are thankful to God. Verbally recount the multitudes of God's mercies in your life and that of your family.

#5. Are there times when you have shown mercy to someone else? How did that make you feel?

"Blessed are the merciful, for they shall obtain mercy." (Matthew 5:7)

#6. For you personally, do you find it easy to both give and receive mercy?

#7. Veteran's Day is November 11th. If you know a Veteran, express your thanks for his or her service to our great country!

The holidays of Thanksgiving and Christmas lend themselves to golden opportunities to exercise mercy and to show that mercy triumphs over judgment.

I'm confident that if your heart is already bathed in God's mercy, He'll dish up some spectacular divine appointments just for you!

Sheila Eismann, Prophetic Seer, Blogger, Author & Teacher, publishes her weekly blog posts endeavoring to encourage others through God's word. Her writings include teaching and instructions on how to apply prophetic insights for daily living.

Please subscribe to receive new blog posts on her website at www.sheilaeismann.com. by clicking the "Subscribe" button in the far upper right-hand corner of her Home webpage.

Sheila Eismann

The Mosaic of Your Life

November 16, 2021

Encouragement

This artistic phrase "The mosaic of your life" has been running through my spirit like a racehorse for a couple of weeks now. It's time to halt the horse, gather my thoughts, and put my fingers to work. It just might be design time for a dose of encouragement!

For you artisans in blogger-reader land, the meaning of the word *mosaic* will be very familiar. Here's a brief refresher for the rest of us. A mosaic is a pattern or picture that is produced by arranging together various colored pieces of sturdy material such as glass, stone, or tile.

https://www.britannica.com/art/mosaic-art is the weblink that describes the history of mosaics for those of you who would like to read all about it.

After the wording "The Mosaic of Your Life" was dropped into my spirit, I drove to town to complete some errands. Much to my surprise, there was a sandwich board on the corner of one of the streets announcing an upcoming class on designing a mosaic from colored glass. Oh, so many opportunities with so few hours in each day! If it's offered again during a non-holiday time frame, I would be interested in attending.

A Small Gift For You DIYers.

If you feel so inclined or get bitten by the art or craft bug over the next few weeks, here's the weblink for how to make a mosaic for beginners if you've not made one in the past.

https://www.instructables.com/How-To-Make-a-Mosaic-For-Beginners/

It might not be a half-bad idea to start with a paper mosaic made from sturdy, colored construction paper before you transition into glass, stone, or tile.

Butterflies Are Blessings.

When selecting the image for this week's prophetic blog post, there were many from which to choose. I purposefully chose this colorful, ornate butterfly.

Butterflies symbolize a new creation, a believer in Jesus Christ, a glorified or heavenly body, changed (from the caterpillar stage to a mature butterfly), soaring in the Spirit, and blessings.

When I would travel periodically with my husband throughout our beloved state, and if it happened to be on a weekend, we would sometimes visit our friends on Sunday morning at the church in Lapwai, Idaho. This geographic location is known as the land of butterflies.

We Are God's Workmanship.

There are physical mosaics and spiritual ones, too.

According to Ephesians 2:8-10, we are God's workmanship.

"For by grace you have been saved through faith, and that not of yourselves; *it is* the gift of God, not of works, lest anyone should boast. For we are His workmanship, created in Christ Jesus for good works, which God prepared beforehand that we should walk in them."

The Greek word for workmanship is *poiema* – Strong's G4161, and it means the works of God as the creator.

https://www.blueletterbible.org/lexicon/g4161/kjv/tr/0-1/

In a spiritual sense, each of us could be considered one of God's mosaics. Since the days of Adam and Eve in the Garden of Eden some 6,000 years ago, can you only imagine how many He would have created by this point in time?

Prophetic Insights For Daily Living.

#1. Have you ever thought of your life as being similar to a mosaic?

_____
_____
_____
_____

#2. A mosaic could be considered a reflection in some ways. As you look back on your life, what would it include? For instance, if you are a teacher, it could include books, a desk, or an apple. An athlete's mosaic might reflect a basketball or a uniform. Mine would certainly include a horse, of course, along with a stack of books, and a predominant theme of the color green as that's my favorite one.

_____
_____
_____
_____

Enlisting the input of others might also help in the design time of your mosaic. Ask them how they view you and your life.

Also, how does your life look differently now as you grow and mature in Jesus Christ (the ultimate metamorphosis process of the butterfly)?

_____
_____
_____
_____

A definite praise is that our mistakes are not included in our life's mosaic if we've accepted Jesus Christ as our personal Lord and Savior and are walking with Him. (Romans 10:9-10) Our assurance comes from Psalm 103:12,

"As far as the east is from the west,

So far has He removed our transgressions from us."

#3. Based upon the Ephesians 2:8-10 verses listed above, we are God's workmanship created in Christ Jesus for good works, that we should walk in them. Our mosaic would include and reflect our God-given destiny and His call upon our life as it pertains to both physical and spiritual giftings and talents. What are your yours?

_____

_____

_____

_____

Studies in ancestral lineages fascinate me in this area. For example, in some families, there are successive generations of preachers, teachers, craftsmen, farmers, tradesmen, etc. It surely sounds like there is a Master Craftsmen busily creating in the heavens!

#4. Art and craft projects can be considered therapeutic exercises. In my prophetic blog post last week, https://sheilaeismann.com/give-receive/, I encouraged readers to serve others with the spiritual gift of mercy.

The Multitude of God's Mercies

Even if you're not the "artsy-craftsy" type, visiting with someone who needs a listening ear will surely make Jesus smile!

#5. Plugging in the symbolism for the accompanying image for this week, the physical and spiritual concepts of blessings are noteworthy studies. There are many Biblical scriptures pertaining to blessings. What is an assuring one that readily comes to you?

_____
_____
_____
_____

When you've prayed for blessings for others or yourself, how has God specifically answered those prayers?

_____
_____
_____
_____

#6. Are there times when you are challenged in the area of being a blessing to someone? The smallest gesture of a kind word or smile can be a HUGE blessing in someone's life. Kind words can remain like sparkling jewels in the heart long after they are spoken. For someone whose love language is words of affirmation, this is especially important.

_____
_____
_____
_____

Blessings don't always have to be material things or something grandiose. If your spirit is stirred this week of how you can bless someone, follow the Holy Spirit's lead as He is the master coordinator and connector. He'll show you exactly what to do. Our cup of blessing continues to be filled as we pour it out to others.

#7. Pray and ask God to show you how He sees you. King David reminds us in Psalm 139:14,

"I will praise You, for I am fearfully *and* wonderfully made;
Marvelous are Your works,

And *that* my soul knows very well."

Just as there are innumerable species of gorgeous and distinct butterflies around the globe, the same applies to each of us. We are uniquely and beautifully created in the image of God. (Genesis 1:26-28)

Celebrate God, Jesus, and The Holy Spirit, and celebrate you because you're one of a kind!

Sheila Eismann, Prophetic Seer, Blogger, Author & Teacher, publishes her weekly blog posts endeavoring to encourage others through God's word. Her

writings include teaching and instructions on how to apply prophetic insights for daily living.

Please subscribe to receive new blog posts on her website at www.sheilaeismann.com. by clicking the "Subscribe" button in the far upper right-hand corner of her Home webpage.

Thanksgiving Traditions

November 22, 2021

Holidays

The Psalmist makes such a joyful announcement to the people of all lands in Psalm 100 which has culminated in Thanksgiving traditions and holiday heritage around the globe for millennia.

"Enter into His gates with thanksgiving,
And into His courts with praise.
Be thankful to Him, *and* bless His name.
For the Lord *is* good;
His mercy *is* everlasting,
And His truth *endures* to all generations." (Psalm 100:4-5)

The 7 commands of Psalm 100.

This passage of scripture is short and sweet but includes some very important reminders of how to worship our God and His Son, Jesus Christ.

Make a joyful shout to the Lord

Serve the Lord with gladness

Come before His presence with singing

Know that the Lord is God

Enter into His gates with thanksgiving

Be thankful to God

Bless the name of the Lord

Traditions are like a double-sided coin.

In Matthew Chapter 15, Jesus confidently answered the scribes and Pharisees' question as to why His disciples transgressed the tradition of the elders. They were all in a huff because Jesus's disciples were not washing their hands before eating bread.

"He (Jesus) answered and said to them, 'Why do you also transgress the commandment of God because of your tradition? For God commanded, saying, *'Honor your father and your mother'*; and, *'He who curses father or mother, let him be put to death.'* But you say, 'Whoever says to his father or mother, "Whatever profit you might have received from me *is* a gift *to God*"— then he need not honor his father or mother.' Thus you have made the commandment of God of no effect by your tradition. Hypocrites! Well did Isaiah prophesy about you, saying:

"'These people draw near to Me with their mouth,
And honor Me with their lips,
But their heart is far from Me.
And in vain they worship Me,
Teaching as doctrines the commandments of men.'" (Matthew 15:3-8)

In a more positive light, the Apostle Paul reminded the church at Thessalonica to stand fast according to the true traditions which he had imparted to them.

"Therefore, brethren, stand fast and hold the traditions which you were taught, whether by word or our epistle." (2 Thessalonians 2:15)

In this passage of scripture, Paul is referencing the revealed, inerrant word of God. He communicated a portion of this to the Thessalonians when he was preaching to them in their midst.

Since the New Testament had not yet been written, the tenants of the Christian faith were communicated via preaching, and writing letters (epistles) to the various churches. The Apostle Paul wrote two-thirds of the New Testament, and the Apostle Peter authored two epistles.

The new believers in Thessalonica were to remain in their belief in Jesus Christ and the gospel of the good news. I have no idea if all of this occurred around the time of our present-day Thanksgiving traditions, but they were to stand fast nonetheless. In essence, this became a positive, new tradition for all of them.

Family Thanksgiving Traditions.

In the image for this week's prophetic blog post, I'm sharing the recipe for Pomegranate Salad which is one of our Thanksgiving Traditions and family faves!

My earliest childhood memories include my sweet mama anxiously awaiting the small, over-taped, brown box full of perfect pomegranates each Thanksgiving.

Lenna Grace, my maternal grandmother who lived to be 89, lived on the Arizona-Nevada border. She was able to procure the very best pomegranates to send to her children who didn't live nearby. After mama unwrapped the package, she drew the fruit close to her face and smiled with pure satisfaction and joy.

The recipe included with this week's blog post is one of my mother's culinary creations.

Another small aspect of this tradition is having the younger kiddos and grandkiddos don some latex gloves and help peel the pomegranates when making the salad. Of course, it helps to have a little extra Cool-whip® for them to sample every now and then, too!

Pomegranate Symbolism.

There are several prophetic symbolisms for pomegranates, but the main ones are as follows:

Healing
Heart
Joyful and fruitful
Fruitful thoughts and a beautiful mind

Prophetic Insights For Daily Living.

#1. Since pomegranates represent healing, is there something in your life that needs to be healed? If so, what is it? Pray and ask God to provide just what you need.

_____
_____
_____
_____

#2. Combining the prophetic symbolism for pomegranates, does your heart need to be healed, physically or spiritually? Make an appointment with Dr. Jesus since He is the great physician. (Mark 2:17)

_____
_____
_____
_____

The soil of a thankful heart produces good and pleasant fruit!

Here's a blog post regarding giving thanks: https://sheilaeismann.com/give-thanks-in-everything/

#3. As you review the 7 aspects of Psalm 100, are there any that you feel you need to ask Jesus to help you with? It's so comforting to know that His mercy is everlasting and His truth endures to all generations.

_____
_____
_____
_____

#4. Who and/or what are you thankful for in your life this year, and why? Oftentimes, it's good to write these down, so you can reflect upon them at a later date. Prophetic journaling is a splendid idea!

_____
_____
_____
_____

#5. I've spoken with a few people lately who have indicated that God is forming or doing something new in their lives. (Isaiah 43:19) Even if it's a pruning of sorts, it can take courage and obedience to be thankful.

#6. What is one of your family's Thanksgiving traditions or holiday heritage? This may be something other than food or special recipes. If you feel so inclined, please leave a comment at the end of this blog post, and share them with us!

_____
_____
_____
_____

#7. Are you feeling a gentle nudge from The Holy Spirit to pen a note or place a call to someone to thank him or her for being in your life?

_____
_____

On the subject of thanksgiving, please know that I'm thankful for each one of you who has either subscribed to my website and taken the time to read my blog posts and make comments or who has purchased one of our books in our shop.

I appreciate all of you and wish you and your family a blessed Thanksgiving. All of us have so much for which to be thankful!

Sheila Eismann, Prophetic Seer, Blogger, Author & Teacher, publishes her weekly blog posts endeavoring to encourage others through God's word. Her writings include teaching and instructions on how to apply prophetic insights for daily living.

Please subscribe to receive new blog posts on her website at www.sheilaeismann.com. by clicking the "Subscribe" button in the far upper right-hand corner of her Home webpage.

Your Spiritual Light Assignment

November 28, 2021

Prophetic Words

Sunday, November 28, 2021, marks the first of the four Sundays of the Advent season. Houses of worship will light their candles preceding the celebration of the birth of our Lord and Savior, Jesus Christ. The candles on the traditional Advent wreath represent hope, love, joy, and peace. They are lit in that exact order, commencing today. This custom is also related to the lighting of the candles celebrating the Feast of Dedication which is also known as the Festival of Lights. The prophetic stirring that I received from The Holy Spirit pertains to your spiritual light assignment during the next month.

Historically speaking, it was during the Feast of Dedication when Jesus initially revealed that He is the Messiah. More importantly, He affirmed that He is God in the flesh which answered the challenge presented to Him as to whether or not He was the Christ. Jesus also spoke one of the greatest assurances of all times to Christian believers in that He is the Shepherd who knows His sheep who hear His voice.

"Now it was the Feast of Dedication in Jerusalem, and it was winter. And Jesus walked in the temple, on Solomon's porch. Then the Jews surrounded Him and said to Him, 'How long do You keep us in doubt? If You are the Christ, tell us plainly.'

"Jesus answered them, I told you, and you do not believe. The works that I do in My Father's name, they bear witness of Me. But you do not believe, because you are not of My sheep, as I said to you. My sheep hear My voice, and I know them, and they follow Me. And I give them eternal life, and they shall never perish; neither shall anyone snatch them out of My hand. My Father, who has given *them* to Me, is greater than all; and no one is able to snatch *them* out of My Father's hand. I and *My* Father are one.'" (John 10:22-30)

God's Omnipotent Light.

We don't have to read too many verses in the first chapter of Genesis to discover the origin of light.

"Then God said, 'Let there be light'; and there was light. And God saw the light, that *it was* good; and God divided the light from the darkness. God called the light Day, and the darkness He called Night. So the evening and the morning were the first day." (Genesis 1:3-5)

Through God's omnipotence, He created light and spoke it into existence. Light is a continued theme from the beginning to end of the Bible:

(a) Genesis 1:3-5 – God created spiritual light. He divided the light from the spiritual darkness.

(b) Genesis 1:14-19 – God created physical light.

(c) John 8:12 – God sent His beloved Son, Jesus Christ, to be the light of the world.

(d) Revelation 21:23 – At the end of this present world, darkness will not exist at all. There will only be light.

It's interesting and noteworthy that the timeframe in which to traditionally light the candles during the Advent season is when it gets the darkest early in our neck of the woods. Sunset is around 5:15 p.m. Alas, after December 21st, the days will begin to lengthen once again.

God exists outside of so many of our earthly dimensions including light and time. I've often wondered if the Apostle John was given revelation at the time of his writings concerning the subject of light. If you read 1 John through 3 John, there appears to be an emphasis upon light. Maybe John was given a glimpse into the spiritual and physical dimensions of light as he penned the words via inspiration from The Holy Spirit.

Prophetic Symbolisms For Light.

Light symbolizes Jesus Christ, God, revelation, illumination, your life, the word of God as a guide (Psalm 119:105), fellowship, walking in the light, God's glory, and a righteous way of living.

Can you think of other aspects of light that are not listed above?

I purposefully chose this week's prophetic blog post image featuring red candles inside the Advent wreath since red is symbolic of Jesus's shed blood on the cross for the remission of our sins.

Perseverance For The Project At Hand.

In parts of the world, some of us are so blessed to live in a dispensation of time where we have access to such everyday conveniences as a light bulb. Here's a link regarding the invention and ongoing development of the different kinds. As you can tell when reading about just one commodity, it took a lot of perseverance to accomplish the projects.

https://www.bulbs.com/learning/history.aspx

Applying a prophetic application, your spiritual light assignment may require a lot of perseverance. "Let us not become weary in doing good, for at the proper time we will reap a harvest if we do not give up." (Galatians 6:9 – NIV)

Here's another blog post with the continued theme of light. This pertained to a prophetic vision I received on September 5, 2021:

https://sheilaeismann.com/new-light/

Candle In The Dark

Prophetic Insights For Daily Living.

#1. **This is a call to action regarding your spiritual light assignment.**

What is the darkest situation, circumstance, or region to which you are being called right now? Is it your:

Family

Yourself

Other Relationships

Neighborhood

Workplace

School

Geographic Region

Or something else?

_____

_____

_____

If you're unaware of any of this or believe it doesn't necessarily pertain to you, pray and ask God to show you. Perhaps you're called to co-labor with someone else and his or her spiritual light assignment.

Teamwork makes the dream work! A three-cord strand is not easily broken, i.e., you, a fellow believer, and Jesus Christ, the light of the world. (Ecclesiastes 3:12 and John 8:12)

Just as God spoke light into existence, pray and ask God to speak light into the darkest situation.

#2. The strategy will not be a one-size-fits-all for your spiritual light assignment. Our internal flame fueled by The Holy Spirit who resides within each of us produces our light flow. Stay closely tuned to His stirrings and directives. Record what is downloaded unto you in your prophetic journal including any specific scriptures and prayer directives. Be mindful to watch for results.

#3. God, Jesus, and The Holy Spirit will be with you in your spiritual light assignment. It's an exciting adventure if you choose to look at it in that light!

John 10:22-30 – Jesus's sheep hear His voice and follow Him. As you listen for His voice, He will impart His strategies to you.

_____
_____
_____
_____

The following are some ways in which God communicates with us:

Dreams

Visions

An audible voice

A voice in your mind or thoughts

Something you just firmly know in your spirit

A prompting or stirring to do or say something

Peace

Divine appointments

Spiritual Songs

A passage of scripture

A sign or wonder – a supernatural event

_____
_____
_____
_____

#4. All of God's creations are initially drawn to His light. Some people will look at a light for a considerable amount of time before they begin to earnestly follow it. This is a good exercise in patience and longsuffering.

_____
_____
_____
_____

#5. The candles on the traditional Advent wreath represent hope, love, joy, and peace. Please plan to walk in these four Christlike virtues as you fulfill your spiritual light assignment. Ask God to fill your light assignment with His omnipotent light. I would encourage you to not stress over the difficulty of your assignment as God will be faithful to release the amount of light needed to help overcome the degree of darkness that is present in the situation.

#6. "You are the light of the world. A city that is set on a hill cannot be hidden. Nor do they light a lamp and put it under a basket, but on a lampstand, and it gives light to all *who are* in the house. Let your light so shine before men, that they may see your good works and glorify your Father in heaven." (Matthew 5:14-16)

In what ways will you let your light shine to others?

May God abundantly bless all of you as you continue to walk in His light during this Advent season and fulfill your spiritual light assignment!

Sheila Eismann, Prophetic Seer, Blogger, Author & Teacher, publishes her weekly blog posts endeavoring to encourage others through God's word. Her writings include teaching and instructions on how to apply prophetic insights for daily living.

Please subscribe to receive new blog posts on her website at www.sheilaeismann.com by clicking the "Subscribe" button in the far upper right-hand corner of her Home webpage.

A Christmas Blessing

December 6, 2021

Holidays

Large, wet snowflakes are falling outside as the savory aroma of homemade split pea soup is wafting throughout our home. While stirring my domestic endeavor, my spirit has been stirred this week with the theme of "A

Christmas Blessing." This is actually tied to our spiritual inheritance if we choose to look at it in that manner.

The most historic and impactful Christmas blessing ever delivered came in the form of a baby born millennia ago in the little town of Bethlehem.

"And it came to pass in those days *that* a decree went out from Caesar Augustus that all the world should be registered. This census first took place while Quirinius was governing Syria. So all went to be registered, everyone to his own city.

"Joseph also went up from Galilee, out of the city of Nazareth, into Judea, to the city of David, which is called Bethlehem, because he was of the house and lineage of David, to be registered with Mary, his betrothed wife, who was with child. So it was, that while they were there, the days were completed for her to be delivered. And she brought forth her firstborn Son, and wrapped Him in swaddling cloths, and laid Him in a manger, because there was no room for them in the inn." (Luke 2:1-7)

Jesus's humble birth may not have seemed significant to most people at the time, but the indelible mark it has left on the world has withstood every challenge and the test of time.

Jesus's Hands & Feet In Action.

When Jesus was instructing His disciples regarding what the kingdom of heaven is like, He spoke of the culmination thereof in Matthew 25:34-36,

"Then the King will say to those on His right hand, 'Come, you blessed of My Father, inherit the kingdom prepared for you from the foundation of the world: for I was hungry and you gave Me food; I was thirsty and you gave Me drink; I was a stranger and you took Me in; I *was* naked and you clothed Me; I was sick and you visited Me; I was in prison and you came to Me.'"

Granted, this worthy instruction carries no expiration date with it; however, the holiday season is an especially important time to keep one aspect of our spiritual inheritance in mind.

How we treat others is the equivalent of the way we would act toward Jesus Himself. To that end, do you deem He throws a test in our paths every now and then to check our hearts and attitudes?

_____
_____
_____
_____

Blessings In The Old & New Testaments.

There are myriads of blessings listed in the Bible from the books of Genesis to Revelation.

The Old Testament Hebrew word for blessing is the feminine noun *beraka* – Strong's H1293. Its meanings are:
Blessing

A source of blessing

Blessing or prosperity

Blessing or praise of God

A gift or present

Treaty of peace

The one reference of this list that piqued my interest was a treaty of peace. Is God calling you to be a Christmas blessing in the form of peace extended to someone?

_____
_____
_____
_____

https://www.blueletterbible.org/lexicon/h1293/kjv/wlc/0-1/

The New Testament Greek feminine noun for blessing is the word *eulogia* – Strong's G2127, from which we derive the word eulogy.

Definitions are as follows:

Praise, laudation, panegyric – of Christ or God

Fine discourse or polished language

In a bad sense, language artfully adapted to captivate the hearer: fair speaking, fine speeches

An invocation of blessing or benediction

Consecration

A (concrete) blessing or benefit

https://www.blueletterbible.org/lexicon/g2129/kjv/tr/0-1/

Prophetic Insights For Daily Living.

#1. Spiritual food for thought: a true test for a true Christian is to love and bless someone when all you have to offer is yourself.

_____
_____
_____
_____

#2. By choosing to be a Christmas blessing, it helps to fill our cup with joy.

#3. During the summer, I authored a prophetic blog post regarding one of the yellow petals on *The Supernatural Hope Flower*. Here's the image and the weblink: https://sheilaeismann.com/grateful-hearts/

Gratitude

#4. What is the **BEST** Christmas blessing that you have ever received?

_____
_____
_____
_____

#5. And what would be the **MOST UNEXPECTED** Christmas blessing that's ever come your way?

_____
_____
_____
_____

#6. I would encourage you to be on the lookout for how you can be a Christmas blessing to someone. For some of you, I deem the Lord may present this in an unconventional manner or avenue. But, that's part of the holiday season fun and spirit, isn't it?

_____
_____
_____
_____

#7. Just for dinner — if you would like to have a copy of my scrumptious Split Pea Soup recipe with its two secret spice ingredients, please send an email to sheila@sheilaeismann.com, and I will be happy to share it with you. Also, there are some delish condiments that you can serve with it. Yum, yum!

A Call to Action.

How do you feel led to be a Christmas blessing to someone else, especially when they have no way to ever repay you? "And whatever you do, do it heartily, as to the Lord and not to men," (Colossians 3:23)

Sheila Eismann, Prophetic Seer, Blogger, Author & Teacher, publishes her weekly blog posts endeavoring to encourage others through God's word. Her writings include teaching and instructions on how to apply prophetic insights for daily living.

Please subscribe to receive new blog posts on her website at www.sheilaeismann.com by clicking the "Subscribe" button in the far upper right-hand corner of her Home webpage.

Sheila Eismann

Joyful

December 13, 2021

Encouragement

Lighting the traditional third candle of joy during this Advent season is far more than just going through the motions. It helps us to focus upon a continued, joyful journey with Jesus Christ, our Lord, and Savior. Oh, that we could be exceedingly joyful in all our tribulation such as the Apostle Paul was when staying in Asia Minor!

"Great *is* my boldness of speech toward you, great *is* my boasting on your behalf. I am filled with comfort. I am exceedingly joyful in all our tribulation." 2 Corinthians 7:4

Paul earnestly cared for the believers at Corinth, but he had to write a stern letter to them admonishing them to repent and turn to God. When they did so, this caused him to be exceedingly joyful.

The Greek word for joyful in the above-listed verse is *chara*, Strong's G5479, which means joy; gladness; the joy received from you; the cause or occasion of joy; or persons who are one's joy.

https://www.blueletterbible.org/lexicon/g5479/kjv/tr/0-1/

Continuing with verses 5-7 of 2 Corinthians 7, "For indeed, when we came to Macedonia, our bodies had no rest, but we were troubled on every side. Outside *were* conflicts, inside *were* fears. Nevertheless God, who comforts the downcast, comforted us by the coming of Titus, and not only by his coming, but also by the consolation with which he was comforted in you, when he told us of your earnest desire, your mourning, your zeal for me, so that I rejoiced even more."

Joy, A Fruit Of The Spirit.

Joy is listed as one of the nine fruits of the Holy Spirit.

"But the fruit of the Spirit is love, joy, peace, longsuffering, kindness, goodness, faithfulness, gentleness, self-control. Against such there is no law. And those *who are* Christ's have crucified the flesh with its passions and desires. If we live in the Spirit, let us also walk in the Spirit. (Galatians 5:22-25)

The challenging aspect about fruit is that it must be nurtured in order to grow. Unfortunately, it's not one of those "Eureka, Overnite" kinds of things that just spring up on their own and are self-maintained.

Inferring from the above scriptures in Galatians, if we're living in the Spirit, we're also walking in the Spirit which means that we are walking in joy.

This will most assuredly help us to

Conquer fear
Erase anxiety
Wash away hopelessness
Infuse hope
Cast our cares upon the Lord and not try to carry them ourselves (1 Peter 5:7)

Stay on the narrow path that leads to everlasting life (Matthew 7:13-14)

Lessons From Mary's Life.

Joy requires follow-through. From the time Jesus's mother, Mary, learned that she was with child until His birth required that she maintain her joy despite challenges along the way. Let's take a look at some of those:

(a) Discovering that she was with child while still in a betrothed state to Joseph.

(b) Receiving and believing what Gabriel, the messenger angel, delivered to her regarding the Christ child.

(c) The arduous journey preceding Jesus's birth was approximately 90 miles, at least a three-day trip via donkey. This was just days before Jesus arrived!

(d) There were no comfortable, heated, cushy birthing rooms in those days such as are available to some women in our modern-day culture. The inn where Jesus was born could well have been a stable for animals or a cave.

(e) Following Jesus's birth, the humble little family would have stayed in Bethlehem for 40 days to fulfill Mary's timeframe of purification under Jewish law. (Leviticus 12:2-4) Following the 40 days, they traveled to Jerusalem to present Jesus to the Lord which was the customary presentation of a firstborn son. (Exodus 13:2, 12)

During this ceremony, a mother could offer either a lamb or two turtledoves (pigeons). Since Joseph and Mary could not afford a lamb, they offered two turtledoves.

Suffice it to say, none of us really know how Mary actually felt about this whole experience. But in my heart, I deem that we can glean a great deal from her joyful song penned in Luke 1:46-55.

But just like Mary, joy will supersede all of life's challenges if we remain in a joyful state.

Endurance Fuels The Joyful Flame.

It can be so hard for us to wrap our minds around the fact that Jesus endured the cross of His crucifixion for the joy that was set before Him. His life's mission was the crown of glory and the reward of heaven. This is the believer's ultimate mission as well.

"Therefore we also, since we are surrounded by so great a cloud of witnesses, let us lay aside every weight, and the sin which so easily ensnares *us*, and let us run with endurance the race that is set before us, looking unto Jesus, the author and finisher of *our* faith, who for the joy that was set before Him endured the cross, despising the shame, and has sat down at the right hand of the throne of God. (Hebrews 12:1-2)

https://sheilaeismann.com/need-more-joy/

Need More Joy

Prophetic Insights For Daily Living.

#1. Being joyful helps us endure our trials and the crosses we must bear. How does this speak to your circumstances at the moment?

_____
_____
_____
_____

#2. Joyfulness is rooted in Jesus and not our situations in life. Do you deem that adopting this mindset helps us to remain victorious during this lifetime?

_____

_____

_____

#3. Focus upon a joyful journey in Jesus Christ. When we concentrate intently upon something, our hearts and feet will follow. It's also contagious, so plan to share your joy with everyone you encounter!

#4. There is joy when we spend time in the presence of the Lord.

Psalm 5:11

Psalm 16:11

Psalm 63:6-7

Psalm 95:1-2

1 Thessalonians 2:19

#5. A joyful life is linked to the God of the impossible Who makes things possible. (Matthew 19:26 and Luke 1:37) What is the number one impossibility in your life right now?

#6. How has remaining joyful helped you? Please plan to share this with others during the Advent season as we prepare to celebrate the reason for the season, Jesus Christ, our precious Lord, and Savior.

My encouragement to all of us this week comes from 1 Thessalonians 5:16-18 in the New Living Translation, "Always be joyful. Never stop praying. Be thankful in all circumstances, for this is God's will for you who belong to Christ Jesus."

Remaining joyful during adverse times speaks volumes as to how much we trust God.

Please continue to pray for all of those in Kentucky and the other states where terrific tornadoes have wreaked such a path of horrific destruction.

Sheila Eismann, Prophetic Seer, Blogger, Author & Teacher, publishes her weekly blog posts endeavoring to encourage others through God's word. Her

writings include teaching and instructions on how to apply prophetic insights for daily living.

Please subscribe to receive new blog posts on her website at www.sheilaeismann.com by clicking the "Subscribe" button in the far upper right-hand corner of her Home webpage.

Prophetic Dream – The P.H.S. & The $325

December 15, 2021
Prophetic Dreams

During the early morning hours of Monday, December 13, 2021, I had a short prophetic dream regarding The P.H.S. and the $325. There were only three scenes in this dream, but I deem that's enough to establish an interpretation thereof. Since finances are one of my wheelhouses, I try to pay close attention when I receive a revelatory download regarding the same.

Scene #1:

I was inside a large building looking for old receipts and gathering up odds and ends of things that belonged to me. A woman named Irene, whose countenance was serious, approached me and said, "A subscription to The Penny Hoarder will be $325.00." I didn't reply to Irene as I thought this was such an odd comment.

Scene #2

Another unnamed woman walked toward Irene and asked her if she would like to go have coffee. The sense I had was that the unnamed woman would be buying coffee for both of them.

Scene #3

In the last scene of the dream, I walked down a small flight of steps as I continued to look for receipts, etc.

End of dream.

Prophetic Symbolism/Thoughts Pertaining To This Short Dream:

#1. P.H.S. = Penny Hoarder Subscription.

#2. It was given to me on the 13th day of December. Thirteen is symbolic of rebellion, sin, backsliding, apostasy, corruption, defection, and depravity.

#3. Here is a link that describes the history of The Penny Hoarder. Its main focus is distributing articles about earning, saving, and managing money.

https://en.wikipedia.org/wiki/The_Penny_Hoarder

Disclaimer regarding The Penny Hoarder: I am merely stating what someone said in a dream.

#4. The meaning of Irene's name is as follows:

"Literal Meaning: Peace (Greek)

Suggested Character Quality: Peaceful Spirit

Suggested Lifetime Scripture Verse: John 14:27, 'Peace I leave with you, My peace I give to you; not as the world gives do I give to you. Let not your heart be troubled, neither let it be afraid.'"

#5. In this dream, I was walking through a building gathering up old receipts and things that belonged to me.

#6. The third, unnamed woman in the dream invited Irene to have coffee with her. Symbolisms for coffee are fellowship and communion; revelation as a stimulant.

Prophetic Insights For Daily Living:

Warning bells have been sounding for quite some time now regarding hyperinflation.

On August 13, 2020, I authored a blog post titled "Prophetic Dream #1 Featuring Silver Coins" which spoke of hyperinflation.

Here's the weblink to revisit it: https://sheilaeismann.com/prophetic-dream-1-featuring-silver-coins/

Prophetic Dream #1 Featuring Silver Coins

#1. If people normally subscribe to The Penny Hoarder to receive insight on how to earn, manage, and save money, the rate of subscribers could skyrocket when hyperinflation really accelerates.

#2. In reviewing the history and background of The Penny Hoarder, I was unable to determine if the publication had always been free. If that was the case, a $325.00 price tag for an annual subscription is quite exorbitant. What this could infer is advertisers are no longer able to place their ads in the publication due to consumers no longer being able to afford their products.

#3. If something that's normally free or sells for a cheap price ultimately skyrockets, how much will a cup of coffee cost?

#4. In this dream, I was rounding up old receipts and things that belonged to me inside a large building. While it's a chore sometimes to retain receipts, this could serve as a reminder, so we don't have to spend time at a later date trying to locate them if necessary.

#5. In the last scene of the dream, I was walking down some steps which indicates losing one's heart in a situation.

#6. God could have placed anyone to speak to me in the dream. The scripture verse accompanying Irene's name reminds us that through Jesus Christ we have peace. Our hearts are not to be troubled or afraid no matter what is going on in the world.

As you read this blog post, what thoughts or directives come to mind?

_____
_____
_____
_____

Bottom Line For This Finance Dream

Regardless of how high inflation soars, Jesus will always be the Prince of Peace, and The Blessed Controller of All things.

Our encouragement comes from Hebrews 13:5, "*Let your* conduct *be* without covetousness; *be* content with such things as you have. For He Himself has said, *"I will never leave you nor forsake you."*

May any economic challenge only increase our faith in Jesus our Lord and His promise to never leave us nor forsake us.

Sheila Eismann, Prophetic Seer, Blogger, Author & Teacher, publishes her weekly blog posts endeavoring to encourage others through God's word. Her writings include teaching and instructions on how to apply prophetic insights for daily living.

Please subscribe to receive new blog posts on her website at www.sheilaeismann.com by clicking the "Subscribe" button in the far upper right-hand corner of her Home webpage.

Christmas Joy

December 21, 2021

Holidays

This beautiful, hand-crafted, Christmas card traveled 7,194 miles before being delivered to our home! It's a highly treasured holiday gift that was prepared by a young boy who's being cared for in one of our church's orphanages. I pray that just looking at this small treasure causes you to smile. May we be possessors and carriers of God's Christmas joy and share it with everyone we meet during this entire holiday season.

I try to watch for developing themes and revelatory messages each year to celebrate our Lord's birth. Last year it was "Comfort at Christmas."

https://sheilaeismann.com/christmas-themes/

Comfort At Christmas

Interestingly enough, this year's theme of Joy and Joyful has appeared in many prophetic ways during the month of December. The most amazing one was via this card featured in this week's prophetic blog post.

Everywhere I've turned or traveled the past few weeks, joy was in my peripheral vision.

#1. When driving into town to complete errands, there was a painted, wooden, spiritual lawn display. Most of these have the word "Believe" placed in the center of them. This one posted the word "Joy."

#2. Our family has a fun, traditional baking day wherein we decorate Christmas cookies and make goodies to give to other family members and friends. I asked our younger grandkiddos to select a Christmas tin for Poppy and me and to fill it with some goodies. I just smiled inwardly when our granddaughter walked into the dining room and handed me a tin that read "Joy" in the center of it. I'd not previously seen the stack of Christmas Tins purchased for the day.

#3. The word "Joy" has appeared on numerous sandwich boards and marquees in our area. In prior years, I've not noticed the repetitive use of this word. Normally, it's "Peace, Love, or Blessings."

#4. The theme of "Joyful" was deposited into my spirit for my weekly blog post on December 13, 2021. This was before we received our hand-crafted Christmas card which just served as a confirmation to me.

#5. One of my favorite things each Christmas season is receiving cards and letters from our family and friends. What's fascinating about the cards that they hand-selected to send us this year is the ongoing theme of joy and joyful!

Prophetic Insights For Daily Living

Heaven help me if this ultra-obvious theme of joy is lost on me as the prophetic signposts are everywhere!

What are some of the ways you've learned to remain joyful during what can sometimes be a stress-filled season?
_____
_____
_____
_____

Staying rooted and grounded in our Lord Jesus Christ, Who is the reason for the season, can definitely keep our "joy barometer" full.

Fill in this sentence, "My Christmas joy would be complete if
_____
_____
_____
_____.

Now, I would encourage you to give this care and concern to The Holy Spirit to carry it for you and to trust God with the outcome.

Walking in joy is a choice just like anything else in life. I can recall a saying from decades ago that went something along the lines of, "Most people are about as happy as they make up their minds to be!" How true is this?

_____

_____

_____

_____

Listening to Christmas carols brings comfort and joy. Music sets a festive holiday tone and uplifts our spirits.

Hope, love, and peace are connected to joy. If any of the first three are out of kilter, joy will most certainly be decreased.

_____

_____

_____

_____

Joy is contagious, so please plan to spread some wherever you go! "A person finds joy in giving an apt reply—and how good is a timely word!" (Proverbs 15:23 NIV)

Please join me in prayer:

Father, we thank You for Your precious Son, Jesus Christ of Nazareth, Who was sent to earth to fulfill the prophecy of Isaiah 9:6-7 and to forgive us of our sins, so we may have eternal life.

As the cares and concerns of this holiday season continue to swirl around us like snowflakes in a windstorm, may we keep our eyes fixed on Jesus Who gives us Christmas joy more abundantly. Let us find joy in the small treasures that You send our way.

To You be the power, glory, and praise, forevermore.

In the mighty name of Jesus, we pray,

Amen, and Amen.

"Now may the God of hope fill you with all joy and peace in believing, that you may abound in hope by the power of the Holy Spirit." (Romans 15:13)

Merry Christmas, everyone & all the best in 2022!

Sheila Eismann, Prophetic Seer, Blogger, Author & Teacher, publishes her weekly blog posts endeavoring to encourage others through God's word. Her writings include teaching and instructions on how to apply prophetic insights for daily living.

Please subscribe to receive new blog posts on her website at www.sheilaeismann.com by clicking the "Subscribe" button in the far upper right-hand corner of her Home webpage.

2022 – The Year of Light

January 1, 2022

Prophetic Teachings

Our outside temperature registered 1 degree on the 1st day of 2022 which made me think of THE most important One, Jesus Christ, our Lord, and Savior. When praying about this new year, I felt directed to study the prophetic symbolism for the number 22 which represents light. As darkness increases, it's definitely time for the year of light to shine brighter than ever before. It's a brand-new day, so let's celebrate God and all of His goodness to us! He's calling us to remain steadfast with optimism in Him.

Children of Light

As Jesus taught on the Mount of Olives, He said,

"You are the light of the world. A city that is set on a hill cannot be hidden. Nor do they light a lamp and put it under a basket, but on a lampstand, and it gives light to all *who are* in the house. Let your light so shine before men, that they may see your good works and glorify your Father in heaven." (Matthew 5:14-16)

Believers in Jesus Christ are called the children of light in 1 Thessalonians 5:5, "You are all sons of light and sons of the day. We are not of the night nor of darkness."

Look For The Lonely

Places of darkness are haunts of cruelty and loneliness. One of the real downsides of the worldwide pandemic has been an alarming rise in people suffering from being alone. This can also lead to destructive side effects.

"God sets the lonely in families, he leads out the prisoners with singing; but the rebellious live in a sun-scorched land." (Psalm 68:6 – NIV)

When trouble arrives on the scene, the result can be for some to quickly isolate themselves. Christians are salt and light who can extend a hand up to connect and go deeper in God and His word. All of us need one another who will stay connected and pray together.

22 Preceded by 20

For this Gregorian calendar year, the year 22 is preceded by the number 20 since we're in the 21st century. For a brief history of why and how we use this system, here's a link for you to take a gander.

https://en.wikipedia.org/wiki/Gregorian_calendar

In prophetic symbolism, the number 20 represents redemption, service, waiting, accountability, responsibility, and expectancy.

Do you deem the aforementioned tie together beautifully with the overall message of children of light looking for the lonely? There's an inherent expectancy for those who God will bring across our path during this year who need redemption, salvation, healing, and deliverance.

Jesus Left The 99

At the beginning of my weekly blog post, I mentioned the number one. Enter the Parable of the lost sheep which Jesus spoke of during His earthly ministry.

"Take heed that you do not despise one of these little ones, for I say to you that in heaven their angels always see the face of My Father who is in heaven. For the Son of Man has come to save that which was lost.

"What do you think? If a man has a hundred sheep, and one of them goes astray, does he not leave the ninety-nine and go to the mountains to seek the one that is straying? And if he should find it, assuredly, I say to you, he rejoices more over that *sheep* than over the ninety-nine that did not go astray. Even so it is not the will of your Father who is in heaven that one of these little ones should perish." (Matthew 18:10-14)

God's will is that no one should perish but come to everlasting life through Jesus Christ His Son. (2 Peter 3:9)

Be Prepared For Your Sychar Moment

The spiritual sense that I have when authoring this message is that some of you may be assigned one particular person during 2022. God will direct every one of your steps, words, and actions if you are submitted to Him. One note of caution is to look inwardly at the person and not at their outward appearance which already could have caused the world to reject or discard him or her.

Please plan to take some time and read John Chapter 4 in your Bible which recounts the story of the Samaritan woman meeting her Messiah. This powerful encounter took place in Sychar, a city in Samaria. At the divine intersection of God's grace, the outcast, a five-time divorcee, became one of the first evangelists in the New Testament.

God, Jesus, and The Holy Spirit never give up on anyone.

Here's the link for one of my blog posts in September of 2020 which you may like to revisit for encouragement.

https://sheilaeismann.com/new-light/

Candle In The Dark

Prophetic Insights For Daily Living

#1. As you read and pray through this message, I would encourage you to make some notes in your prophetic journal regarding how the Holy Spirit is stirring your spirit. Record any scriptures that He quickens unto you.

_____
_____
_____
_____

#2. During an anointed year of light, God will also be shining His light within us presenting a challenge to make inward changes according to His word, if applicable.

_____
_____
_____
_____

#3. In what areas of your life is God calling you to remain steadfast with optimism in Him?

_____
_____
_____
_____

#4. Do you know of anyone who has isolated himself or herself? Is God leading you to leave the 99 and seek out the one?

_____
_____
_____
_____

#5. Are your heart and spirit ready for those who God will divinely bring across your life intersection of redemption and friendship?

_____
_____
_____
_____

#6. Have you prepared for your "Sychar Moment?" This can certainly take some spiritual growth and super-stretching as we cast off old mindsets and preconceived ideas.

_____
_____
_____
_____

Please join me in praying,

"Father,

Thank You for this new year of 2022.

I choose to place my hand in Yours and walk with you every day.

May Your watchful eye rest upon me at all times

As I continue in Your kingdom along the way.

My encouragement for this year comes from Your Word which stands firm in the heavens and does not sway.

Through Your light, increase our light within,

That we may search for the lost before they fade away.

We pray this in the mighty name of Jesus Christ, the name that is above every name.

Amen."

Sheila Eismann, Prophetic Seer, Blogger, Author & Teacher, publishes her weekly blog posts endeavoring to encourage others through God's word. Her writings include teaching and instructions on how to apply prophetic insights for daily living.

Please subscribe to receive new blog posts on her website at www.sheilaeismann.com by clicking the "Subscribe" button in the far upper right-hand corner of her Home webpage.

Our Sustenance Word

January 9, 2022

Prophetic Teachings

Have you noticed that life doesn't unfold so that we're guaranteed to have 365 stress-free, fun-filled, non-worry days? There will definitely be some of those in the mix, but not in totality. Just as the mixing of dough took place to create the above-featured loaves of bread, my spirit has been stirred of late regarding our individual sustenance word for 2022 and the importance of relying upon the Bread of Life.

We're only eight (8) days into our new Gregorian year, and I've found myself repeatedly turning the pages of my Bible to Psalm 37:3-4,

"Trust in the Lord, and do good;
Dwell in the land, and feed on His faithfulness.
Delight yourself also in the Lord,
And He shall give you the desires of your heart."

One thing I particularly like and appreciate about these two verses is the five, progressive steps.

#1. Trust

#2. Do good

#3. Dwell in the land

#4. Feed on His faithfulness

#5. Delight yourself also in the Lord

A little ditty of, "These five things," has also been running through my spirit like a racehorse. God, Jesus, and The Holy Spirit are wanting me to focus upon these verses and get them deeply ingrained into my mind and heart.

Preserving, Sustaining, and Reviving.

When consulting the spiritual definition of the word sustenance, I was greatly encouraged at my find. The Hebrew word for sustenance is *mihya* (Pronounced mikh-yaw), Strong's H4241, which carries the following meanings:

preservation of life

sustenance

reviving

the quick of the flesh, live flesh, tender or raw flesh

https://www.blueletterbible.org/lexicon/h4241/kjv/wlc/0-1/

There's an emphasis upon preserving, sustaining, and reviving.

Jesus Relied Upon His Sustenance Word.

Before Jesus began His earthly ministry and just after His baptism in the Jordan River, He was providentially led by the Spirit into the wilderness to be tempted by the devil.

After fasting forty days and nights, the devil appeared to Jesus to command that He turn stones into bread to prove that He was the son of God.

Jesus, full of The Holy Spirit without measure, relied upon one of His sustenance words, *"It is written, 'Man shall not live by bread alone, but by every word that proceeds from the mouth of God.'"* (Matthew 4:4; accord Deuteronomy 8:3)

Our Bread of Life, Jesus Christ Our Lord and Savior.

Reading in the gospel of John, we find that the *Bread of Life* is one of the titles that Jesus uses to describe Himself. It is one of several "I Am" statements that He implements throughout this book of the New Testament.

"And Jesus said to them, 'I am the bread of life. He who comes to Me shall never hunger, and he who believes in Me shall never thirst.'" (John 6:35)

While sitting on a mountain, Jesus looked below at the multitudes who had gathered to hear Him as they sat in the grassland. He took five loaves of bread and two small fish with which He fed thousands of people. There were twelve baskets of leftover food when it was all said and done.

That same night, Jesus walked on water.

With the Holy Spirit still drawing, wooing, and gathering, those same thousands of people gathered again the next day to be fed. It's at this point that Jesus offers them salvation through Him which is nourishment for eternity.

Do you think the people would have returned the following day if their physical needs had not first been met?

_____

_____

_____

_____

_____

Jesus Christ of Nazareth and the Word of God are not only our temporary sustenance but more importantly, our eternal one.

Have you ever had the opportunity to meet someone's physical needs initially and then present the gospel to them? If so, what was the result?

_____

_____

_____

_____

If Your Boat Begins to Rock, Jesus Will Be With You.

Years ago, some of our family members took a vacation to northwestern Wyoming. We rented a canoe to spend the day on Jackson Lake.

When we were in the middle of the lake, suddenly, a windstorm came out of nowhere, and our canoe began to rock back and forth.

Jesse Amos Obadiah, our little Jack Russell Terrier, was in the canoe with us. Jesse wasn't calm on a good day, much less on this particular one. He began jumping all over the canoe as I desperately clamored to keep him and me inside of it!

Jackson Lake, Wyoming

The squall didn't last too long, but I did find myself calling out to Jesus during the storm. I prayed and asked Him to command the winds and the waves to obey Him as I drew upon this Biblical account,

"On the same day, when evening had come, He said to them, 'Let us cross over to the other side.' Now when they had left the multitude, they took Him along in the boat as He was. And other little boats were also with Him. And a great windstorm arose, and the waves beat into the boat so that it was already filling. But He was in the stern, asleep on a pillow. And they awoke Him and said to Him, 'Teacher, do You not care that we are perishing?'

"Then He arose and rebuked the wind, and said to the sea, 'Peace, be still!' And the wind ceased and there was a great calm. But He said to them, 'Why are you so fearful? How is *it* that you have no faith?' And they feared exceedingly, and said to one another, 'Who can this be, that even the wind and the sea obey Him!'" (Mark 4:35-41)

When speaking to His disciples, Jesus challenged them regarding their faith. It's as if time has stood still on this subject. There have been times when I've felt like my faith is challenged every day. In November of 2020, my weekly blog post was centered on this subject. https://sheilaeismann.com/lifes-puzzle/

The Missing Piece

The Word of God Is Living And Active.

"For the word of God *is* living and powerful, and sharper than any two-edged sword, piercing even to the division of soul and spirit, and of joints and marrow, and is a discerner of the thoughts and intents of the heart." (Hebrews 4:12)

If you have not yet received your sustenance word for 2022, pray and ask God to give you one as only He knows what lies ahead for you this year. Thankfully, He knows the end from the beginning. (Isaiah 46:10)

Our best day and our worst one.

No matter what happens on any given day, may we be reminded to go back to our sustenance word. It needs to become deeply imprinted into our spirit to preserve and revive us (two of the definitions of *mihya,* the Hebrew word for sustenance).

Our sustenance word works for both types of days and everything in between.

Prophetic Insights For Daily Living

#1. Just like Jesus was able to combat the devil with one of His sustenance words, God will do the same for us if we are attacked by the enemy of our souls.

#2. Our physical bodies need nourishment to survive. The same applies to our spirits since we are created as triune people with body, soul, and spirit. Praise God that His word has been preserved and translated down through the millennia, so we can hold a written Bible in our hands today!

#3. Is there anyone you know who does not have a Bible of his or her own? Pray about gifting a new one to someone to provide spiritual sustenance to them.

#4. How has Jesus been with you in the storms of your life?

#5. If we feel ourselves starting to drift when challenges come our way, our sustenance word can help draw us back to the true magnetic north which is God and His word.

#6. Have you ever turned to God's word to sustain you?

#7. As you read this encouraging word, what scriptures and thoughts are quickened unto you? Please make note of them in your spiritual diary or prophetic journal.

#8. As the new year dawns, I would invite you to leave a comment to share about your sustenance word. This helps to encourage all of us. The rising tide benefits all ships!

May God preserve, sustain, and revive you with His word,

Fill you to overflowing with His love,

Bless you abundantly with His peace and presence,

Hold you tightly in His everlasting arms,

As you press in and trust Him with every aspect of your daily life.

A Call to Action:

Pray and ask the Lord to show you someone to whom you can gift a loaf of bread that you have baked or purchased from a grocery store. If this person has not already accepted Jesus Christ as his or her personal Lord and Savior, plan to share the good news of the gospel and watch what happens!

Sheila Eismann, Prophetic Seer, Blogger, Author & Teacher, publishes her weekly blog posts endeavoring to encourage others through God's word. Her writings include teaching and instructions on how to apply prophetic insights for daily living.

Please subscribe to receive new blog posts on her website at www.sheilaeismann.com. by clicking the "Subscribe" button in the far upper right-hand corner of her Home webpage.

The One Who Is With Us

January 16, 2022

Encouragement

After Jesus sat down with His twelve apostles, He instituted the Lord's supper. Fellow Christians around the world still commemorate this act in remembrance of our Lord and will do so until He returns. It was in this setting that Jesus warned of His betrayer. After the apostles discussed who among them would do such a thing, they began to argue as to who was the greatest among them.

Jesus instructed them concerning servanthood and afterward encouraged them with a wonderful promise. Just as Jesus needed men to be with Him in His trials, He is the One Who is with us during our trials. Granted, we know this, but when the fat really hits the fire, it's such a comfort to remember this guarantee and the future promise it holds for the most important wedding of all time.

"But you (the twelve apostles) are those who have continued with Me in My trials. And I bestow upon you a kingdom, just as My Father bestowed *one* upon Me, that you may eat and drink at My table in My kingdom, and sit on thrones judging the twelve tribes of Israel." (Luke 22:28-30)

Since we're not one of the original twelve apostles from millennia ago, we'll not be sitting on thrones judging the twelve tribes of Israel, but we will be eating and drinking with Jesus, our Bridegroom, at the Wedding Supper of the Lamb if we have accepted Him as our personal Lord and Savior before we pass away.

Partaking of communion regularly helps us to continually anticipate the day in which we will be able to celebrate with Jesus our Lord at this all-important marriage feast.

https://sheilaeismann.com/clues-in-communion-bread/

The Four Communions

The Wedding Supper of The Lamb.

Jesus is the Lamb of God and the Bridegroom.

"The next day John (the Baptist) saw Jesus coming toward him, and said, Behold! The Lamb of God who takes away the sin of the world!'" (John 1:29; Revelation 6:16; 12:11; 17:14; 21:27 and 22:3)

"And Jesus said to them (John the Baptist's disciples), 'Can the friends of the bridegroom mourn as long as the bridegroom is with them? But the days will come when the bridegroom will be taken away from them, and then they will fast.'" (Matthew 9:15; Mark 2:19-20; Luke 5:34-35; John 3:29; and 2 Corinthians 11:2)

Believers in Christ, the church, are His bride.

"Husbands, love your wives, just as Christ also loved the church and gave Himself for her, that He might sanctify and cleanse her with the washing of water by the word, that He might present her to Himself a glorious church, not having spot or wrinkle or any such thing, but that she should be holy and without blemish." (Ephesians 5:25-27)

Two Parables For Double Emphasis.

Thankfully, we are given clear instructions from Jesus in the gospel of Matthew about preparing for and receiving our invitation to the great feast ahead of time. In both of these settings, Jesus is addressing the chief priests and elders of the people. Interestingly, He taught this vital lesson with back-to-back parables.

#1. The Parable of the Tenants, a/k/a The Wicked Vinedressers. (Matthew 21:33-44)

#2. The Parable of The Wedding Feast at Matthew 22:1-14,

"And Jesus answered and spoke to them again by parables and said: 'The kingdom of heaven is like a certain king who arranged a marriage for his son, and sent out his servants to call those who were invited to the wedding;

and they were not willing to come. Again, he sent out other servants, saying, 'Tell those who are invited, 'See, I have prepared my dinner; my oxen and fatted cattle *are* killed, and all things *are* ready. Come to the wedding.' But they made light of it and went their ways, one to his own farm, another to his business. And the rest seized his servants, treated *them* spitefully, and killed *them*. But when the king heard *about it,* he was furious. And he sent out his armies, destroyed those murderers, and burned up their city. Then he said to his servants, 'The wedding is ready, but those who were invited were not worthy. Therefore go into the highways, and as many as you find, invite to the wedding.' So those servants went out into the highways and gathered together all whom they found, both bad and good. And the wedding *hall* was filled with guests.

"But when the king came in to see the guests, he saw a man there who did not have on a wedding garment. So he said to him, '**Friend**, how did you come in here without a wedding garment?' And he was speechless. Then the king said to the servants, 'Bind him hand and foot, take him away, and cast *him* into outer darkness; there will be weeping and gnashing of teeth.' (Emphasis mine)

"For many are called, but few *are* chosen.'"

Both of the aforementioned teachings help believers, the Bride of Christ, to ultimately prepare to meet and dine with their Bridegroom.

It's so encouraging that a wedding invitation is being extended to those who have yet to come into the kingdom of God through His Son, Jesus Christ of Nazareth. (John 3:16 and Romans 10:9-10)

When reading through this parable, I was especially struck by the word **_Friend_** at Matthew 22:12.

The Greek word for friend in this verse is *hetairos* (pronounced het-ah'-ee-ros), Strong's G2083. The meanings are a comrade, mate, partner, in kindly address, and friend (my good friend).

https://www.blueletterbible.org/lexicon/g2083/kjv/tr/0-1/

In the parable, Jesus immediately spotted the man who was not wearing the proper garment. Thankfully, the word of God includes instructions for how to clothe ourselves with the Lord Jesus Christ and His imputed righteousness.

"But put on the Lord Jesus Christ, and make no provision for the flesh, to *fulfill its* lusts." (Romans 13:14)

Colossians 3:12-17 speaks of the characteristics of a new person in Jesus Christ and putting on the equivalent of Christlike garments.

A Future Glimpse Into The Wedding Hall

While he was exiled on the Isle of Patmos, the Apostle John was given the privilege of hearing and seeing the multitudes who were in heaven praising God at the Wedding Supper of the Lamb.

"Let us be glad and rejoice and give Him glory, for the marriage of the Lamb has come, and His wife has made herself ready. And to her, it was granted to be arrayed in fine linen, clean and bright, for the fine linen is the righteous acts of the saints.

"Then he said to me, 'Write: 'Blessed *are* those who are called to the marriage supper of the Lamb!' And he said to me, 'These are the true sayings of God.'" (Revelation 19:7-9)

The Great Commission Goes Hand-in-Hand With The Wedding Invitation.

"Then the eleven disciples went away into Galilee, to the mountain which Jesus had appointed for them. When they saw Him, they worshiped Him; but some doubted.

"And Jesus came and spoke to them, saying, 'All authority has been given to Me in heaven and on earth. Go therefore and make disciples of all the nations, baptizing them in the name of the Father and of the Son and of the Holy Spirit, teaching them to observe all things that I have commanded you; and lo, I am with you always, *even* to the end of the age. Amen.'" (Matthew 28:16-20)

Jesus's command to go and make disciples of all nations is a double invitation in that acceptance of the first one leads to the assurance of the second one which is the Wedding Supper of the Lamb. We can only imagine what it will be like to finally meet the One Who Is With Us on earth as it will be in heaven. What a joyous occasion and feast that will be!

Prophetic Insights For Daily Living.

#1. Have you accepted your invitation of believing in Jesus Christ as your personal Lord and Savior? (Romans 10:9-10)

_____

_____

_____

#2. Is there anyone that God is laying upon your heart to share the good news, i.e., the gospel of His Son, Jesus Christ, to assure a seat inside the Wedding Feast?

_____

_____

_____

#3. Try to imagine what the Wedding Supper of the Lamb will be like!

#4. Were Jesus's words to His disciples acknowledging their reward for staying with Him in His trials a surprise to you?

#5. Just as there will be rewards for Jesus's apostles for continuing with Him, there will be different types of rewards for us according to 1 Corinthians 3:5-15.

#6. What type of trial are you or someone you know enduring right now? How have you been led to comfort and encourage them?

I'm extremely grateful for the One Who Is With Us, and I would like to close this week's blog post with some comforting words from the Apostle Paul penned to the church at Corinth,

"Blessed *be* the God and Father of our Lord Jesus Christ, the Father of mercies and God of all comfort, who comforts us in all our tribulation, that we may be able to comfort those who are in any trouble, with the comfort with which we ourselves are comforted by God." (2 Corinthians 1:3-4)

Sheila Eismann, Prophetic Seer, Blogger, Author & Teacher, publishes her weekly blog posts endeavoring to encourage others through God's word. Her writings include teaching and instructions on how to apply prophetic insights for daily living.

Sheila Eismann

The Year of God's Rainbow

January 22, 2022
Prophetic Visions

Who among us doesn't enjoy gazing at a beautiful rainbow in the sky? Amid winter where so much of our nation is experiencing life in the deep freeze, ice storms, whiteouts, power outages, etc., this recent prophetic vision was most encouraging. On Friday, January 14, 2022, I was spending some quiet time with the Lord. Suddenly, a rainbow manifested in the Spirit with 2022 supernaturally spread over it. This isn't just any old rainbow. I knew by revelation that this is the year of God's rainbow.

At the start of each new Gregorian year, there are many prophetic words and themes that emerge. As I pray into them, I look for confirmations and parallels.

Prophetic Symbolisms.

When the spirit realm opened on the fourteenth, I knew immediately that it pertained to deliverance as this is one of the symbols for the number 14. Others are liberty; the Passover which was instituted on the 14th of the Hebrew month Nisan (Exodus 12:1-20); and a double measure of spiritual perfection.

I would encourage you to read the 9th chapter of Genesis where we initially see God's rainbow appear.

Rainbows represent God's covenant promise to us as believers; God's glory; a Heavenly vision; and remembrance.

God's rainbow, the seal of the Noahic Covenant, was not only a symbol of God's covenant to man but also to beasts and the earth itself. That's quite an all-encompassing promise and covenant!

God's promises.

One of the most often quoted scriptures in the Bible regarding promises can be found at 2 Corinthians 1:20, "For all the promises of God in Him *are* Yes, and in Him Amen, to the glory of God through us."

In the opening chapter of this book, the Apostle Paul recounts his comfort from suffering, being delivered from suffering, and admonishing the body of believers at Corinth.

While there can be a tendency to "paint with a very broad brush" when reciting the above verse to apply it to whatever we would like to have in this present life, that's not exactly what it means.

The secret lies in verse 19 which states, "For the Son of God, Jesus Christ, who was preached among you by us—by me, Silvanus, and Timothy—was not Yes and No, but in Him was Yes."

The explanation of 2 Corinthians 1:20 is that Jesus Christ is the same yesterday, today, and forever. (Hebrews 13:8) This is such assurance for Christians today and God's promise that we can surely stand upon. It will help us to stay anchored in Him and not be blown about by every strange wind of doctrine.

God's Bow & God's Rainbow.

When researching the use of the word *rainbow* in the Bible, I found that it was used only twice in the New Testament in the book of Revelation.

The Greek word for rainbow is *iris* (pronounced ee'-ris), Strong's G2463.

Iris caught my eye, no pun intended. Anatomically speaking, the iris is the colored portion of the eye that helps to regulate the amount of light that enters the eye. It's a pigmented curtain whose job is to monitor the amount of light. When there's a bright light, the iris closes the pupil to let in less light, and when there's lower light, the iris expands the pupil to allow more light to enter. Humans are very complex creatures and fearfully and wonderfully made. (Psalm 139:14)

Revelation 4:3 describes Jesus Christ, our precious Lord and Savior, as sitting on the throne in heaven with a rainbow surrounding it. The rainbow reflects the beams of the Sun of Righteousness who comes with healing in His wings. (Malachi 4:2)

At Revelation 10:1, the Apostle John describes the mighty angel with the little book. "I saw still another mighty angel coming down from heaven, clothed with a cloud. And a rainbow *was* on his head, his face *was* like the sun, and his feet like pillars of fire."

https://www.blueletterbible.org/lexicon/g2463/kjv/tr/0-1/

Strong's H7198, *queset*, (pronounced keh'-sheth) is the Hebrew word for bow or rainbow and is found 76 times in the Old Testament. It first appears in Genesis 9:13. The meanings are a bow (for hunting and battle), bowmen, archers, used figuratively as might, and rainbow.

https://www.blueletterbible.org/lexicon/h7198/kjv/wlc/0-1/

For those of us with grandiose imaginations, it's as if God strings His bow and shoots His rainbow into the sky at the precise moment that we need to see it!

Prophetic Promises.

In the book of 1st Timothy, the Apostle Paul pens a letter to Timothy to instruct him to stay in Ephesus to safeguard the pure gospel teachings. Toward the end of this, Paul encourages him to fight the good fight of faith. "This charge I commit to you, son Timothy, according to the prophecies previously made concerning you, that by them you may wage the good warfare, having faith and a good conscience, which some having rejected, concerning the faith have suffered shipwreck." (1 Timothy 1:18-19)

From these two verses, we can infer that there had previously been prophetic promises given concerning Timothy and his ministry. We learn from these scriptures that we must contend for and wage warfare concerning the prophetic words that we have received.

We don't know exactly how it was that the Apostle Paul had knowledge of this information, but in his apostolic role, he committed this all-important charge to Timothy.

ROYGBIV

In April 2021, I received a prophetic vision wherein I saw several sets of hands holding light blue, matching knitting needles. Next, I heard a clicking sound. The hands would knit for a few minutes and stop. Then they would start again.

The sense I had was the knitting pertained to corporate, intercessory prayer wherein the intercessors were being given downloads or burdens to pray simultaneously as they were knitting together God's plans. There's was a clarion call to action as not everything was as it seemed in the natural realm during that time frame.

ROYGBIV is the acronym for the colors of the rainbow which are red, orange, yellow, green, blue, indigo, and violet. God was calling His intercessors to the 7 mountains of culture, society, and influence.

https://sheilaeismann.com/call-to-action/

Knitting Together God's Plans

Prophetic Insights For Daily Living.

#1. Have you received any type of prophetic promises in the past that have yet to be fulfilled? If so, you may need to continue to war over them just like the Apostle Paul instructed Timothy. (1 Timothy 1:18-19) To that end, stand on God's promises, continue to pray and seek His face, and follow His lead and instructions.

_____
_____
_____
_____

#2. I would encourage you to start a Promise Journal for 2022 and record how God leads and answers you throughout the year. I still have prayer journals from 30 years ago that I can reflect upon for continued encouragement and revisit God's faithfulness.

_____
_____
_____
_____

#3. When reading Genesis 9, what spoke to you from this passage of scripture, or how was your spirit stirred?

_____
_____
_____
_____

#4. Just as the rainbow is a sign of God's covenant, do you need to renew your covenant relationship with Him? He is so forgiving, merciful, loving, and kind and does not want anyone to perish without having eternal life. (2 Peter 3:9)

_____
_____
_____
_____

#5. The number 14 represents deliverance. Is there something in your life that you need to be delivered from or do you know someone who needs deliverance? God is not only a God of promises but also of deliverance from anything that keeps us in sin and from fully loving and serving Him. Life on earth is not about perfection because there was only one perfect man, Jesus Christ of Nazareth.

_____
_____
_____
_____

https://www.biblestudytools.com/topical-verses/bible-verses-on-deliverance is a helpful resource for verses regarding this subject matter.

#6. In what areas do you or someone you know need God's promises from His word? The more time we spend with Him and reading our Bible, the more promises we will discover which can help to build our faith immensely.

_____
_____
_____
_____

Meditating upon the promises of God brings us much joy.

The rainbow symbolizes covenant. In 2022, God is emphasizing that we need to renew our covenant with Him. As we read and study the Old Testament, we discover there were times when God allowed severe weather storms, famines, and pestilences to get the Israelites' attention, so they would turn back to Him. This is the year to turn back to God, if applicable.

Noah found grace in the eyes of the Lord. (Genesis 6:8) God's grace is extended to us each and every day through His precious Son, Jesus Christ of Nazareth, to strengthen and/or renew our relationship with Him or accept Jesus as our Lord and Savior for the very first time.

Watch for God's rainbows during 2022. According to Matthew 19:26, nothing is impossible with Him. He just might surprise us with a double rainbow right in the middle of a snowstorm. Wouldn't that be awesome? Let's keep our eyes on the promises of God!

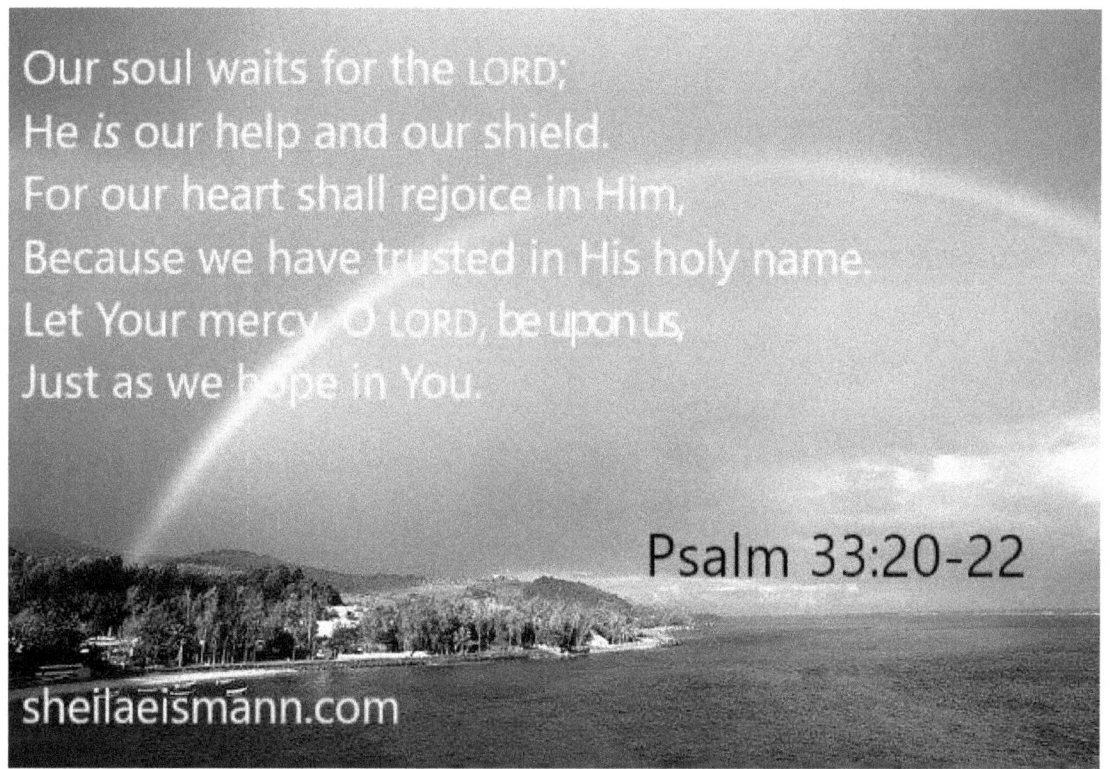

Sheila Eismann, Prophetic Seer, Blogger, Author & Teacher, publishes her weekly blog posts endeavoring to encourage others through God's word. Her writings include teaching and instructions on how to apply prophetic insights for daily living.

Prophetic Dream – The Book Cover

January 29, 2022

Prophetic Dreams

God will sometimes use the everyday things in our lives and weave them into our dreams during the night season. Such was the case early Tuesday morning, January 25, 2022. For the past couple of weeks, I'd been collaborating with a few of my fellow creative authors to plan for some upcoming February book specials.

During that time, we had exchanged images of book covers via email. This must have still been resonating through my spirit when I received the prophetic dream about the book cover.

Decoding dreams can be spiritually rewarding and challenging. According to Genesis 40:8, dream interpretations belong to God. Through the power of the Holy Spirit, He will help us to interpret the dreams that He gives us.

Scene #1.

In the first scene, a hardbound book cover appeared in front of me. There was nothing and no one else around. Similar to some cover designs these days, the author's name was listed first in a large, bold, black font. A much smaller one portrayed the title of the book.

Disclaimer: I am merely recounting a dream that was given to me. I don't know anyone in real life named Rachel Donovan.

Much to my surprise, when completing some internet research, I found a link to an author named Rachel Donovan who has authored a book titled *He Is Enough: God Needs People Who Don't Scare Easily.*

https://www.amazon.com/He-Enough-Needs-People-Easily/dp/0996255613

Scene #2.

A young thirtyish-aged woman was hurriedly walking down a city street in the Autumn of the year. I did not recognize the geographic area. She was heavily concentrating upon the dark brown and rusted gold deciduous leaves that were swirling around her ankles. She was wearing a skirt, blouse, and light overcoat, so she may have been trying to get back home after work before the storm arrived. I knew by revelation the woman walking was not the author of the book.

End of dream.

Marrying Up The Meanings of The Names.

If you've had the opportunity to read some of my prophetic blog posts in the past, you know that I especially enjoy solving a prophetic puzzle that is given to me via a dream or vision. Using my Biblical resources and interpretive books, I explore every angle that I can as I'm directed by The Holy Spirit. To that end, I checked on the meanings of the names Rachel and Donovan.

"Rachel:

Literal Meaning: Little Lamb

Suggested Character Quality: Little Lamb

Suggested Lifetime Scripture Verse: Isaiah 40:11, 'He will feed His flock like a shepherd; He will gather the lambs with His arm, And carry *them* in His bosom, *And* gently lead those who are with young.'"

"Donovan:

Literal Meaning: Dark Warrior

Suggested Character Quality: In God's Light

Suggested Lifetime Scripture Verse: Matthew 5:16, 'Let your light so shine before men, that they may see your good works and glorify your Father in heaven.'"

Among several other emerging themes and emphases, 2022 is the year of light. My first blog post of the new year addressed this all-important subject.

2022 – The Year of Light

https://sheilaeismann.com/remain-steadfast/

Prophetic Symbols To Implement Dream Decoding.

The dream was given to me on the 25th day of the month. Twenty-five symbolizes the forgiveness of sins; expecting the grace or mercy of God; being brought to account by the grace of God; and grace upon grace.

Book has quite a few symbols such as a literal book; words; contract; meditate; and your life plan. The most relative one I located was the individual and his or her heart.

This dream took place in the Autumn of the year as evidenced by the deciduous leaves swirling around the woman's ankles. Autumn represents moving toward winter; fading away; the end; sin or being carried away. It's also interesting that the wind was causing the leaves to swirl around the woman as she walked.

Ankles symbolize a person's faith or spiritual walk; base or foundation; preaching the gospel with strength, and support or new standing.

Leaves represent words as in "leaves of a book;" pages; a person's life; new life; righteous life; living a fearful life; and evergreen life. Dead leaves are symbolic of dead words and without fruit.

Scripture Verses Emphasized.

While praying into, studying, researching, and preparing this week's blog post, these are the scriptures that were emphasized to me by The Holy Spirit.

John 20:30-31, "And truly Jesus did many other signs in the presence of His disciples, which are not written in this book; but these are written that you may believe that Jesus is the Christ, the Son of God, and that believing you may have life in His name."

Romans 10:6-13, "But the righteousness of faith speaks in this way, '*Do not say in your heart, 'Who will ascend into heaven?*' (that is, to bring Christ down *from above*) or, '*Who will descend into the abyss?*' (that is, to bring Christ up from the dead). But what does it say? '*The word is near you, in your mouth and in your heart*' (that is, the word of faith which we preach): that if you confess with your mouth the Lord Jesus and believe in your heart that God has raised Him from the dead, you will be saved. For with the heart one believes unto righteousness, and with the mouth confession is made unto salvation. For the Scripture says, '*Whoever believes on Him will not be put to shame.*' For there is no distinction between Jew and Greek, for the same Lord over all is rich to all who call upon Him. For '*whoever calls on the name of the Lord shall be saved.*'"

Hebrews 5:12-14, "For though by this time you ought to be teachers, you need *someone* to teach you again the first principles of the oracles of God; and you have come to need milk and not solid food. For everyone who partakes *only* of milk *is* unskilled in the word of righteousness, for he is a babe. But solid food belongs to those who are of full age, *that is,* those who by reason of use have their senses exercised to discern both good and evil."

Revelation 21:27, "But there shall by no means enter it (the New Jerusalem) anything that defiles, or causes an abomination or a lie, but only those who are written in the Lamb's Book of Life."

Prophetic Insights For Daily Living.

#1. After pondering this dream, how does it speak to you? Please record this in your prophetic journal if you've started one. These can become wonderful teaching tools as you deepen your walk with the Lord and partner with the Holy Spirit in decoding your dreams.

_____
_____
_____
_____

#2. As you read each of the emphasized scripture verses, what was quickened unto you?

_____
_____
_____
_____

#3. Considering the accompanying scripture verse for Rachel's name in this dream, have you accepted Jesus Christ as your personal Lord and Savior, so your name is already written in the Lamb's book of life?

#4. Reinforcing Donovan's lifetime scripture verse, there is a special anointing from God helping you to let your light shine before men. (Matthew 5:16) People are drawn to the light, and there may be wonderful opportunities for you to share the good news, the gospel of Jesus Christ, during 2022.

#5. In the dream, the dead leaves were swirling around the young woman's ankles. Her focus was upon this and not looking straight ahead to where she was going. Ankles symbolize a person's spiritual walk and dead leaves are dead works and without fruit. She was walking, living her life, in ankle-deep, dead fruit.

This serves as a relevant reminder to examine our spiritual walk to determine if it's bearing fruit.

#6. As the kingdoms of this world continue to shake, there's definitely an urgency of the hour for salvation. In God's infinite mercy, He's not willing that any should perish, but all should come to everlasting life. (2 Peter 3:9) A double confirmation of this is the dream was given to me on the twenty-fifth day of the month with 25 symbolizing the forgiveness of sins through Jesus's atoning death on the cross. There's grace upon grace for our sins.

#7. Pray and ask God for opportunities and open doors to share the gospel message. When visiting with a Christian sister and prayer partner last week, she told me that she felt directed by The Holy Spirit to include a salvation message in her Christmas cards and letters. It's important to remember that it's our responsibility to share the gospel and leave the outcome to God. Jesus is our Shepherd, and we are the sheep of His pasture who hear His voice. (John 10:11 and 14)

As strange as it may seem, some people do not believe in an afterlife at all. They've either been taught or through self-reason have arrived at the opinion that this present earth is all there will ever be.

In a nutshell, I'm confident this is the reason I received this short dream bearing the subtitle of the book to remind people that there is absolutely an afterlife.

Of all the books we will ever read in this lifetime, the Bible is by far the most important one. Happy Reading!

"For whatever things were written before were written for our learning, that we through the patience and comfort of the Scriptures might have hope." (Romans 15:4)

Sheila Eismann, Prophetic Seer, Blogger, Author & Teacher, publishes her weekly blog posts endeavoring to encourage others through God's word. Her writings include teaching and instructions on how to apply prophetic insights for daily living.

Please subscribe to receive new blog posts on her website at www.sheilaeismann.com. by clicking the "Subscribe" button in the far upper right-hand corner of her Home webpage.

Sheila Eismann

Sign In The Sky

February 4, 2022

Prophetic Teachings

As portrayed in the accompanying image to my weekly prophetic blog post, a heavenly portal certainly invaded the earth before the sun slipped over these desert mountains! My field of vision is supernaturally parked in the burning orange center of this gorgeous photo which bears a strong resemblance to a cross. With increasing frequency, God is continuing to speak His heavenly language via a sign in the sky.

Perhaps King David of the Old Testament was gazing at the night sky when he penned the following verses,

"The heavens declare the glory of God;
And the firmament shows His handiwork.
Day unto day utters speech,
And night unto night reveals knowledge.
There is no speech nor language
Where their voice is not heard.
Their line has gone out through all the earth,
And their words to the end of the world.
In them He has set a tabernacle for the sun,
Which *is* like a bridegroom coming out of his chamber,
And rejoices like a strong man to run its race.
Its rising *is* from one end of heaven,
And its circuit to the other end;
And there is nothing hidden from its heat." (Psalm 19:1-6)

The people who reside in or visit Arizona can probably attest to the fact that there's nothing hidden from its heat!

My husband had an annual speaking engagement for a couple of decades in Phoenix during August. I don't think that even the lizards and other desert creatures can withstand the sweltering heat during the days of that month, much less the inhabitants.

When we visited Phoenix, misters lined the city streets attempting to cool everyone and everything down. That gives a new definition to the old one-liner, "It's a 110 in the shade and no shade!"

The Hebrew word for firmament in Psalm 19 is *raqia* (pronounced *raw-kee'-ah* – Strong's H7549) which means "properly, an expanse, i.e. the firmament or (apparently) visible arch of the sky:—firmament."

https://www.blueletterbible.org/lexicon/h7549/kjv/wlc/0-1/

The arch of this particular Yuma night firmament was beyond visible bearing an important sign in the sky.

This spectacular imagery was captured by our friends Timm and Ronda who are wintering in sunny Arizona. When Timm first saw this appear in the night sky, he commented, "Looks like a portal to heaven!"

The beauty of portals is that they can instantly seize our attention, connect with our spirits, and remind us of God's magnificent creation.

A portal is an open heaven, gate of heaven, doorway, or entry point where heaven and earth intersect or meet. It's quite often a place of increased angelic activity and where heaven invades the earth realm. It affords a spherical opening/portal of light that offers divine protection and assistance through which heavenly beings can freely come and go without any demonic hindrance.

Heavenly Portals.

Genesis 28 establishes the account of Jacob experiencing a heavenly portal.

"Now Jacob went out from Beersheba and went toward Haran. So he came to a certain place and stayed there all night, because the sun had set. And he took one of the stones of that place and put it at his head, and he lay down in that place to sleep. Then he dreamed, and behold, a ladder *was* set up on the earth, and its top reached to heaven; and there the angels of God were ascending and descending on it.

"And behold, the Lord stood above it and said: 'I *am* the Lord God of Abraham your father and the God of Isaac; the land on which you lie I will give to you and your descendants. Also your descendants shall be as the dust of the earth; you shall spread abroad to the west and the east, to the north and the south; and in you and in your seed all the families of the earth shall be blessed. Behold, I *am* with you and will keep you wherever you go, and will bring you back to this land; for I will not leave you until I have done what I have spoken to you.'

"Then Jacob awoke from his sleep and said, 'Surely the Lord is in this place, and I did not know *it*.' And he was afraid and said, 'How awesome *is* this place! This *is* none other than the house of God, and this *is* the gate of heaven!'" (Genesis 28:10-17)

This scriptural account reinforces some very important points.

#1. In Jacob's dream, he saw the angels ascending and descending to heaven. God kept all demonic interference away from this heavenly portal during this spiritual encounter.

#2. God spoke to Jacob in the dream to confirm the Abrahamic Covenant. (Genesis 12:1-3)

#3. After this encounter, Jacob definitely realized it was a gate or portal of heaven and declared it to be so.

#4. How would you like to use a stone for a pillow?

_____
_____
_____

#5. It's instructive to note that a supernatural ladder was provided for angels to ascend and descend. They were not flying through the air in this particular instance.

#6. Jacob was not able to walk up the ladder to heaven.

In the New Testament, we find a verbal exchange between Jesus and Nathanael.

"Nathanael answered and said to Him, 'Rabbi, You are the Son of God! You are the King of Israel!'

"Jesus answered and said to him, 'Because I said to you, 'I saw you under the fig tree,' do you believe? You will see greater things than these.' And He said to him, 'Most assuredly, I say to you, hereafter you shall see heaven open, and the angels of God ascending and descending upon the Son of Man.'" (John 1:49-51)

Fast forward to the book of Revelation, and the Apostle John experienced a heavenly door or portal to receive the revelation of Jesus Christ and His return during the end times.

"After these things I looked, and behold, a door *standing* open in heaven. And the first voice which I heard *was* like a trumpet speaking with me, saying, 'Come up here, and I will show you things which must take place after this.'

"Immediately I was in the Spirit, and behold, a throne set in heaven, and *One* sat on the throne. And He who sat there was like a jasper and a sardius stone in appearance; and *there was* a rainbow around the throne, in appearance like an emerald. Around the throne *were* twenty-four thrones, and on the thrones I saw twenty-four elders sitting, clothed in white robes; and they had crowns of gold on their heads.

And from the throne proceeded lightnings, thunderings, and voices. Seven lamps of fire *were* burning before the throne, which are the seven Spirits of God." (Revelation 4:1-5)

In the next four verses of Revelation Chapter 4, the Apostle John continues to describe what he saw and heard via this heavenly portal.

Substantiated Spiritual Activity.

The portals are heavenly openings that touch the earth in various locations to enable angelic and spiritual activity which release salvations, healings, miracles, signs and wonders, and prophetic revelation.

In retrospect, we can see this confirmed through some of the great Christian revivals in past eras such as the Welsh Revival during 1904-1905. This was the largest one recorded during the 20th century. Right on the heels of this was the famous Azusa Street Revival in Los Angeles, California, which began on April 9, 1906, and continued until approximately 1915.

Walking & Co-Laboring with The Holy Spirit.

When we accept Jesus Christ as our personal Lord and Savior, we receive the indwelling of the Holy Spirit Who is the deposit guaranteeing our heavenly inheritance.

"In Him you also *trusted,* after you heard the word of truth, the gospel of your salvation; in whom also, having believed, you were sealed with the Holy

Spirit of promise, who is the guarantee of our inheritance until the redemption of the purchased possession, to the praise of His glory." (Ephesians 1:13-14).

As we walk, co-labor, and partner with The Holy Spirit, He reveals the open heavens, portals, and doorways.

Increased Angelic Activity.

In speaking with fellow Christians of late, there's an alarming increase in angelic activity in the form of supernaturally hearing doorbells ring, someone knocking at the door, packages being scanned, etc. during the night season. People are in a very deep sleep and are suddenly awakened to these manifestations and are recording them. Also, people are capturing unique cloud formations such as eagles flying in the sky.

God's Paintbrush.

Here's a sunrise image I captured on an early November 2020 morning in a different desert setting. While it's not nearly as stunning or carries the prophetic message as the one from Timm and Ronda, it reminds us of God's majestic artistry.

God's Paintbrush

Here's the link to read the prophetic weekly blog post that accompanied this early Autumn picture: https://sheilaeismann.com/sunrise/

Prophetic Insights For Daily Living:

#1. Just as Jesus challenged Nathanael in the Biblical account from the first chapter of the gospel of John, He is reminding non-believers today of His atoning death on the cross. (1 Corinthians 15:3; Romans 5:8; 1 Peter 3:18;

and Hebrews 9:15) Perhaps that is one of the main reasons for the Yuma sunset bearing the image of the cross.

_____

_____

_____

_____

#2. If you carefully study this photo from Timm and Ronda, at the center of the cross you can see a wavy, orange, vertical line descending toward the middle mountain.

_____

_____

_____

_____

This reinforces the heavenly portal or open heaven. It's so exciting that our friends were in the right place at the right time!

#3. Every once in a while, I can detect a major shift in my prophetic writing assignments from the Lord. This has been true of late with an urgent theme of salvation. God is not willing that any should perish but that all should come to everlasting life. (2 Peter 3:9)

_____

_____

#4. God is no respecter of persons. (Acts 10:34 and Romans 2:11) We are carriers of His glory, and His Holy Spirit resides within each of His believers. We are assured according to Hebrews 1:3 that Jesus is the radiance of God's glory. If we have accepted Jesus Christ as our personal Lord and Savior, He is with us, and the glory of God resides within us.

#5. How do this prophetic blog post and the glorious sign in the Yuma sky speak to you?

#6. I started reading a book this past week in which the very first line read, "I wonder what it's like to die." Believers in Jesus Christ of Nazareth don't need to wonder or worry about this. We have the assurance from the Apostle Paul in 2 Corinthians 5:1-8.

#7. If the Holy Spirit is laying someone upon your heart to share the salvation message, gift a Bible, pray with them, etc., please follow through with that prompt, nudge, or stirring.

Look up, keep your eyes on the Prize, Jesus Christ of Nazareth, and release His glory everywhere the soul of your foot treads upon!

Every day holds the possibility of miracles, supernatural encounters, and open heavens.

Sheila Eismann, Prophetic Seer, Blogger, Author & Teacher, publishes her weekly blog posts endeavoring to encourage others through God's word. Her writings include teaching and instructions on how to apply prophetic insights for daily living. Please subscribe to receive new blog posts on her website at www.sheilaeismann.com. by clicking the "Subscribe" button in the far upper right-hand corner of her Home webpage. (I met Timm & Ronda in the 1990s at a small, country church in the desert. God still keeps us connected in His divine grace and love.)

Sheila Eismann

Double Bloom ~ Double Portion

February 11, 2022

Encouragement

Holly is still so happy! Look at this gorgeous, pink, double bloom. In all of the years that we've owned our Christmas Cactus, she's never produced something like this. When I walked closer to our fireplace mantle to address Holly for the day and thank her for adding joy to our lives, I heard in the Spirit, "Double bloom, double portion."

It's fascinating how God can and will use the everyday things in our lives to convey what's on His heart.

Double Bloom, Double Portion, & Double Scriptures.

When I consulted the word of God for the exact wording of "double portion," I found that it only appears twice.

The first instance is in Deuteronomy 21:17, and secondly in 2 Kings 2:9, "And so it was, when they had crossed over, that Elijah said to Elisha, 'Ask! What may I do for you, before I am taken away from you?'

"Elisha said, 'Please let a double portion of your spirit be upon me.'"

Year Two Of The Decade of Pey.

On God's calendar, we're in the Hebrew year of Bet which is year two of the decade of Pey. Yes, we function in the Gregorian calendar, but it's God's timeframe that always takes precedence.

Here's a real nugget that's buried deep in the Bible: the Hebrew word for portion as in double portion is *pe* (pronounced *peh*), Strong's H6310. So, it's the same Hebrew word for portion as is the entire decade from 2020 through 2030!

The various meanings are:

Peh – mouth
Mouth (of man)
Mouth (an organ of speech)
Mouth (as of animals)
Mouth, opening, orifice (of a well, river, etc.)
Extremity, end.

https://www.blueletterbible.org/lexicon/h6310/kjv/wlc/0-1/

The Fruit of Our Lips.

"Therefore by Him let us continually offer the sacrifice of praise to God, that is, the fruit of *our* lips, giving thanks to His name." (Hebrews 13:15)

Proverbs 18:21, "Death and life are in the power of the tongue: and they that love it shall eat the fruit thereof."

It would appear as though the more we praise and thank Holly, the more prolifically she blooms! She usually starts her blooming cycle in early November and continues through April or May of each year.

Holly is Happy in February

Blooms are symbolic of abundance, joy and rejoicing, harvest time, chosen by God, fruitfulness, and beauty.

Quoting from Cathie Richardson, a beautiful, talented artist regarding Cactus which represents ardent love, endurance, and warmth.

"The cactus flower colors have different meanings. The white and yellow blooms symbolize strength and endurance. The pink and orange blooms symbolize youth. The cactus flower message is to not let the world bring you down. Everything you need is inside of you, and you can produce beautiful things in the middle of an empty desert."

A couple of things really resonate with me from the above description. Holly bears pink blooms which represent youth.

Regarding youthfulness, Isaiah 40:31 comes to mind,

"But those who wait on the Lord
Shall renew *their* strength;
They shall mount up with wings like eagles,
They shall run and not be weary,
They shall walk and not faint."

We live in the desert, so we know the inherent challenges that come with it. I'm encouraged by Cathie's words, "Everything you need is inside of you, and you can produce beautiful things in the middle of an empty desert." With God's help, we can produce what it is that He's calling us to do." We will continue to blossom!

For a real treat, I would encourage you to purchase Cathie's beautifully illustrated book titled *Victorian Flora: A Language of Flowers Handbook*. Here's the link:

https://www.amazon.com/Victorian-Flora-Language-Flowers-Handbook-ebook/dp/B0848PS4N6/ref=sr_1_1?crid=1D89K9YQMO7D8&keywords=cathie+richardsons+book+victorian+flora&qid=1644349374&sprefix=cathie+richardsons+book+victorian+flora%2Caps%2C139&sr=8-1

Plan to spend some time perusing her artistry and the accompanying descriptions for the various flowers. I'm enlightened each time I read through Cathie's book.

2022 – The Year of Light.

My first prophetic blog post of the year expanded upon 2022 being the year of light. One of the reasons Holly is still blooming is because of the light in the window above our fireplace.

Things in the natural realm will mirror those of the spiritual realm, and vice-versa, even if it's through a cactus!

New Beginnings in Adar.

Holly's double bloom first appeared on February 8, 2022. Eight is symbolic of new beginnings, new strength, superabundance (double of anything good usually is), worshipping God, and regeneration.

February 8, 2022, falls on the 7th day of the Hebrew month of Adar which means strength and represents the completion of the season.

Adar is the month of joy and a time for rejoicing over God's victories in your life. It's a great time to revisit and study the book of Esther where God granted His people victory over their enemies.

There are so many verses in the Bible that contain the word joy. Find your favorite one and memorize it during the month of Adar.

Also, here's a short, sweet blog post I've previously written regarding joy.

https://sheilaeismann.com/fill-your-cup-with-joy/

Prophetic Insights For Daily Living.

#1. This is the year to ask God for a double portion of His Holy Spirit to rest upon you, manifest in you, and speak through you. The Biblical example of this can be found in 2 Kings 2:9 when "Elisha said, 'Please let a double portion of your spirit be upon me.'"

_____
_____
_____
_____

#2. The Biblical month of Adar is also the month for your true spiritual identity to be revealed to the world. Stir up your God-given gifts and bless those around you with them. The spiritual gifts are listed in Romans 12:3-8; 1 Corinthians 12:1-11; and Ephesians 4:7-16.

#3. As I'm preparing this week's prophetic blog post, I'm sensing a caution in the area of expectation. In other words, allow God to be large and in charge in your life. If the double portion doesn't emerge in the area in which you deem it should, don't give up on God! Just as there are late bloomers in life as the old saying goes, just maybe where you've been sowing might bloom later than you think.

#4. It's a constant challenge to guard our mouths and try to control what emerges from them. I wonder how often King David prayed this prayer from verses 3-4 of Psalm 141,

"Set a guard, O Lord, over my mouth;
Keep watch over the door of my lips.
Do not incline my heart to any evil thing,
To practice wicked works
With men who work iniquity;
And do not let me eat of their delicacies."

#5. Is there a particular area of your life where you would like to receive a double portion? Submit your request to God as He already knows the desires of your heart. Watch with expectancy to see how He answers your specific prayer.

_____
_____
_____
_____

#6. If you might be experiencing joylessness, pray and ask God to show you what's robbing you of your joy. We all go through valleys and mountain top experiences in this lifetime, but even in the midst of these, we can still experience God's joy.

_____
_____
_____
_____

"But let all those rejoice who put their trust in You;
Let them ever shout for joy, because You defend them;
Let those also who love Your name be joyful in You." (Psalm 5:11)

Sheila Eismann, Prophetic Seer, Blogger, Author & Teacher, publishes her weekly blog posts endeavoring to encourage others through God's word. Her

writings include teaching and instructions on how to apply prophetic insights for daily living.

Please subscribe to receive new blog posts on her website at www.sheilaeismann.com. by clicking the "Subscribe" button in the far upper right-hand corner of her Home webpage.

No Early Retirement

February 18, 2022

Prophetic Teachings

Numbers have fascinated me for quite some time now, especially if they happen to appear in sequence or a repetitive fashion. On February 12, 2022, at 11:22 p.m., "Occupy Till I Come" was deposited into my spirit. Early retirement is typically associated with one's vocation or profession; however, according to God's word, there's no such thing in a spiritual sense.

In the 19th chapter of Luke, we are introduced to Zacchaeus, a man of short stature, who was the chief tax collector in Jericho. He was viewed as persona non grata by his fellow Jews because he was a Roman Empire tax collector.

Those serving in these positions typically enriched themselves by running less than an honorable business. When collecting the taxes, some of them would either add more than the exacted amount or pocket some of the funds after wringing it out of the residents. This elevated the term *self-enrichment* to a whole new level even if it was 1.5 millennia ago.

The shady connotation surrounding tax collectors could well explain why Zacchaeus, despite being short, climbed into a sycamore tree to see Jesus as he passed by. The Lord ultimately proclaimed salvation had come to Zacchaeus's house, so all is well that ends well. (Luke 19:1-10)

"Occupy Till I Come."

To continue with what was deposited into my spirit late in the evening of February 12, 2022, let's revisit the Biblical account commencing in verse 11 of Luke 19,

"And as they heard these things, he (Jesus) added and spake a parable, because he was nigh to Jerusalem, and because they thought that the kingdom of God should immediately appear.

He said therefore, A certain nobleman went into a far country to receive for himself a kingdom, and to return.

And he called his ten servants, and delivered them ten pounds, and said unto them, Occupy till I come.

But his citizens hated him, and sent a message after him, saying, We will not have this *man* to reign over us.

And it came to pass, that when he was returned, having received the kingdom, then he commanded these servants to be called unto him, to whom he had given the money, that he might know how much every man had gained by trading.

Then came the first, saying, Lord, thy pound hath gained ten pounds.

And he said unto him, Well, thou good servant: because thou hast been faithful in a very little, have thou authority over ten cities.

And the second came, saying, Lord, thy pound hath gained five pounds.

And he said likewise to him, Be thou also over five cities.

And another came, saying, Lord, behold, here is thy pound, which I have kept laid up in a napkin:

For I feared thee, because thou art an austere man: thou takest up that thou layedst not down, and reapest that thou didst not sow.

And he saith unto him, Out of thine own mouth will I judge thee, thou wicked servant. Thou knewest that I was an austere man, taking up that I laid not down, and reaping that I did not sow:

Wherefore then gavest not thou my money into the bank, that at my coming I might have required mine own with usury?

And he said unto them that stood by, Take from him the pound, and give it to him that hath ten pounds.

(And they said unto him, Lord, he hath ten pounds.)

For I say unto you, That unto every one which hath shall be given; and from him that hath not, even that he hath shall be taken away from him.

But those mine enemies, which would not that I should reign over them, bring hither, and slay *them* before me." (Luke 19:11-27 – KJV)

This passage of scripture is typically referred to as the Parable of the Minas or Parable of the Talents.

Two Parables With A Different Background.

— In the Luke 19:11-27 account, Jesus spoke the parable as he neared Jerusalem because most Jews thought that the kingdom of God should immediately appear in the form of a political ruler instead of a spiritual one.

Luke 19:12 reinforces that the nobleman (Jesus) went into a far country to receive for himself a kingdom and to return.

— Jesus also teaches about the Parable of the Talents in Matthew 25:14-30. He does so in the context of explaining what the Kingdom of Heaven is like and setting the stage for His ultimate crucifixion, ascension, and second return as King of Kings and Lord of Lords. It's during this time that each person will be rewarded for what they've done with their talents.

During Old Testament times, talent was the unit of measurement for weighing the various precious metals such as gold and silver. In The New Testament, a talent referred to a specific value of money or a coin which was the equivalent of about 6,000 denarii. A denarius was a day's wage for a common laborer. (Matthew 20:2) For those of you who enjoy a mathematical challenge, you could calculate what one talent would be worth in today's market.

The word *occupy* as in "Occupy Till I (Jesus) Come" means to invest with the absolute intent of increase.

The Greek word is pragmateuoma (pronounced prag-mat-yoo'-om-ahee), Strong's G4231, and means to be occupied in anything, to carry on a business, to carry on the business of a banker or a trader.

https://www.blueletterbible.org/lexicon/g4231/kjv/tr/0-1/

I deem this is especially applicable in the Luke 19 wording since it parallels Zacchaeus and his vocation as a tax collector. Jesus would often use the things of everyday life to portray important spiritual lessons and principles.

Where are we to invest or trade in? It's the kingdom of God of which there is a multitude of places to plant, water, cultivate, weed, and harvest.

Back to my reference of early retirement if that's even possible for most people these days in light of a continuing worldwide pandemic, these double parables are speaking of being spiritually productive until Jesus calls us home to be with Him.

There are natural, earthly, physical businessmen and women. What these combined verses are addressing is the charge to all of us to be dutiful and diligent spiritual business people. Any spiritual thing God has blessed us with or called us to can and should be multiplied for His kingdom's purposes. How does it get multiplied? By using it!

Matthew 25:18 mentions the third servant who dug a hole in his backyard and buried it. The outcome of this wasn't really pleasant as only the first two servants were rewarded for their efforts.

What About All Those Two's Paired With That Eleven?

Since I received this spiritual reminder at 11:22 p.m. on February 12, 2022, that's 6 two's and one eleven.

In Biblical symbolism, the number two represents a repetitive situation; witness (as in the testimony of two witnesses in Deuteronomy 19:15 and 2 Corinthians 13:1); division; separation; association or agreement; reward or increase; double-mindedness; or second heaven.

Eleven represents judgment; disorder; incompleteness; and imperfections.

What's intriguing about these numbers and their meanings is how it relates to The Parable of the Talents. In this parable, Jesus speaks of the reward or increase (one of the meanings of the number two) and there will be judgment (represented by the number eleven) how we used the talents that have been issued to us on judgment day after He returns.

The Negative Twins.

Doubt and discouragement can sometimes knock on the doors of our hearts as the negative twins. For the past couple of years, there have seemed like times when they've broken down the doors and rushed in like a flood.

Closing the doors to these two, if applicable, and opening the ones for faith and hope, we can return to the Father's kingdom business.

On April 5, 2021, I published a prophetic blog post about the Parable of the Talents. Here's the link: https://sheilaeismann.com/the-parable-of-the-talents/

The Woman, The Wishing Well, & 1932

Prophetic Insights For Daily Living:

#1. What are some of the practical, spiritual ways that you are spending your talents for the kingdom of God?

_____
_____
_____
_____

#2. How does this week's prophetic blog post speak to you or stir your spirit?

_____
_____
_____
_____

#3. We know some dear Christian friends who have come alongside a man they befriended decades ago when both of them were public school teachers. Fast forward to now, and the man is all alone and very limited in a physical capacity. Our friends make it a point and have carved time from their overflowing weekly schedule to help this man with his needs, take him out to lunch, round up his supplies, and show him unconditional love.

_____
_____
_____
_____
_____
_____

#4. A ministry of encouragement is vital every day and can be exercised by a phone call, card in the mail, email, text message, or be creative!

_____
_____
_____

#5. Seek God concerning the continued increase of your spiritual talents. Unlike having physical currency in the bank these days which is not bearing much interest at all, exercising our talents is collecting much heavenly increase.

#6. If you're unsure of how you can fulfill Jesus's teaching in these two parables, enlist the assistance of a trusted spiritual advisor or

Christian friends. Christianity is a team sport, and teamwork makes the dream work.

#7. In the hustle, bustle, confusing, demanding world in which we find ourselves, may we all continue to value our Lord Jesus Christ, His kingdom, and what it is that He has entrusted to us to steward. When the battles heat up, what we value most can become tarnished like old, antique coins. While they might be worth some physical currency these days, the real prize is the spiritual type. Let's keep our gaze fixed upon that.

This week's prophetic blog post is not intended to lay a guilt trip on anyone at all. Its sole purpose is a word of encouragement for all of us to "Occupy Till I (Jesus) Return" and a hefty reminder that there's no early retirement!

Drill deep into the word of God and follow the Holy Spirit's leading. Both of these will serve as a guaranteed spiritual road map to help make you a profitable servant.

_____
_____
_____
_____

"And whatever you do, do it heartily, as to the Lord and not to men, knowing that from the Lord you will receive the reward of the inheritance; for you serve the Lord Christ." (Colossians 3:23-24)

Sheila Eismann, Prophetic Seer, Blogger, Author & Teacher, publishes her weekly blog posts endeavoring to encourage others through God's word. Her writings include teaching and instructions on how to apply prophetic insights for daily living.

Please subscribe to receive new blog posts on her website at www.sheilaeismann.com. by clicking the "Subscribe" button in the far upper right-hand corner of her Home webpage.

NJD – Don't Quit!

February 25, 2022

Prophetic Dreams

Vince Lombardi, one of the greatest professional football coaches of all time, coined the phrase, "Winners Never Quit, And Quitters Never Win." On the heels of my recent prophetic blog post about the Parable of the Talents, I received a prophetic vision and dream which reinforce the theme of Don't Quit! We must continue to run the race set before us.

There are short or lengthy seasons wherein revelatory downloads can be given to us in spiritual patterns. This seems to be the case lately where I've received dreams and visions using people's names. Thus far, they have been people who I don't know in real life, except for the doctor in my recent dream.

Earlier this week, the name Norma Jean Davenport, NJD, appeared in the Spirit. Following this, the wording "Don't Quit!" was impressed upon me.

Important Disclaimer:

If your name is Norma Jean Davenport in real life, be encouraged, and may God richly bless you and your family!

Norma's name:

"Literal meaning: A Rule; A Pattern or Precept

Suggested Character Quality: Examples of Godliness

Suggested Lifetime Scripture Verse: 1 Timothy 4:8, "For bodily exercise profits a little, but godliness is profitable for all things, having promise of the life that now is and of that which is to come."

Jean's name:

"Literal meaning: God is Gracious

Suggested Character Quality: God's Gracious Gift

Suggested Lifetime Scripture Verse: Isaiah 30:18,

"Therefore the Lord will wait, that He may be gracious to you;
And therefore He will be exalted, that He may have mercy on you.
For the Lord *is* a God of justice;
Blessed *are* all those who wait for Him."

The surname Davenport:

"English: habitational name from a place in Cheshire named Davenport, from the Dane river (apparently named with a Celtic cognate of Middle Welsh dafnu 'to drop', 'to trickle') + Old English port 'market town'."

https://www.google.com/search?q=meaning+of+the+name+davenport&rlz=1C1CHBF_enUS800US801&oq=meaning+of+the+name+Davenport&aqs=chrome.0.0i512j0i390l4.3460j0j7&sourceid=chrome&ie=UTF-8

When I think of the word davenport, which is another name for an upholstered couch or sofa, it reminds me of a piece of furniture where you might recline in your living room. The name comes from a 19th century Massachusetts furniture maker, A.H. Davenport, and Company.

Nowadays, we refer to them as couches or sofas, but when I was growing up, they were called davenports.

Decoding NJD ~~ Norma Jean Davenport:

A pattern of Godliness through His gracious gift as we wait for His justice while periodically resting on a davenport.

When you study the combined meanings of these three names, what speaks to you?

Dr. Paula & The Prophetic Dream.

During the early morning hours of February 23, 2022, I received a short dream wherein I'd gone to see a doctor I know in real life named Paula. Much to my surprise, she said she needed to examine my legs which was not the reason for my initial appointment.

After looking at my legs, Paula didn't say there was anything wrong with them.

End of dream.

Paula's name:

"Literal meaning: Little

Suggested Character Quality: Dependent on God

Suggested Lifetime Scripture Verse: Psalm 73:28,

"But *it is* good for me to draw near to God;

I have put my trust in the Lord God,

That I may declare all Your works."

The prophetic symbolism for legs speaks of our spiritual walk; strength and power; support; and running our Christian race.

A doctor represents Jesus, the Great Physician; the need to seek God for healing; Holy Spirit balm; authority; or sickness.

Also, the healing Balm of Gilead is one of the symbols for a doctor. In ancient times there came from Gilead, beyond the Jordan River, a natural substance used for healing. It was derived from a tree or shrub and was a major commodity of trade in the ancient world. There are many substances used today which have been implemented from the natural realm such as Aspirin from willow bark.

When writing to the New Testament church at Corinth, the Apostle Paul questioned them, "Do you not know that those who run in a race all run, but one receives the prize? Run in such a way that you may obtain *it*." (1 Corinthians 9:24) The prize to which he is referring is the crown of eternal life. (James 1:12; 1 Peter 5:4; 2 Timothy 4:8; and Revelation 2:10)

Patience is the key to running our eternal race per Hebrews 12:1, "Therefore we also, since we are surrounded by so great a cloud of witnesses, let us lay aside every weight, and the sin which so easily ensnares *us*, and let us run with endurance the race that is set before us."

The race that is set before us is an endurance race like a marathon, not a sprint. One of my brothers-in-law was a long-haul trucker for decades. We've got to stay in the kingdom of God for the long haul.

Don't Quit! would be like sitting down instead of keeping running. We need to keep walking out our lives daily with God and run the race that is set before us. It's hard to run a race if we're sitting on a davenport or couch!

Also, if we quit on God and do not depend upon Him, how can we declare all of His works and receive the promise of eternal life? (Paula's Suggested Character Quality and Lifetime Scripture Verse of Psalm 73:28)

As we continue to testify what God has done for us and is presently doing, it stirs the hearts of believers and non-believers. It could well open the door of salvation for some who need to come into the kingdom of God before it's too late.

Psalm 22:22 "I will praise you to all my brothers; I will stand up before the congregation and testify of the wonderful things you have done." (TLB)

"Come *and* hear, all you who fear God,
And I will declare what He has done for my soul." (Psalm 66:16)

Dr. Paula Dream Deciphered.

Drawing near to God, depending upon Him, declaring His works through our lives as we run the race set before us to receive the crown of eternal life.

The Holy Spirit is our Paraclete.

The Holy Spirit is the third person of the trinity (Matthew 28:19) Who dwells within us (1 Corinthians 3:16).

John 14:26 (KJV) speaks of the Holy Spirit as the Comforter.

"But the Comforter, *which is* the Holy Ghost, whom the Father will send in my name, he shall teach you all things, and bring all things to your remembrance, whatsoever I have said unto you."

The word *Comforter* in the above verse is *Parakletos* Strong's G3875, which has the basic meaning of "calling to one's side" for help when needed.

Back to the prophetic dream where I'd gone to see Dr. Paula who examined my legs, with legs symbolizing our walk, the Holy Spirit is our paraclete Who walks beside us.

Prophetic Insights For Daily Living.

#1. How many of you have felt like quitting lately as it pertains to the things God is calling you to do or complete? If so, have you been able to discern the reason(s) for this?

_____

_____

During some seasons of life, maturity is in the waiting.

The Maturity Is In The Waiting

https://sheilaeismann.com/freedom-from-anxiety/

#2. Are you waiting for some type of justice in your life (based upon the accompanying scripture verse for Jean's name – Isaiah 30:18, "For the LORD is a God of justice.")?

#3. James 4:8 reminds us to draw near to God, and He will draw near to us. When the storm clouds roll in, we definitely need to be near God. (Psalm 91)

#4. Pray and ask God to help you with boldness and encouragement, so you don't quit.

#5. If you are continuing with your prophetic journaling, look up scriptures pertaining to encouragement and record them. Here are some to render assistance:

1 Samuel 30:6, "Now David was greatly distressed, for the people spoke of stoning him, because the soul of all the people was grieved, every man for his sons and his daughters. But David strengthened himself in the LORD his God."

Isaiah 41:10, "Fear not, for I *am* with you;
Be not dismayed, for I *am* your God.
I will strengthen you,

Yes, I will help you,
I will uphold you with My righteous right hand."

Galatians 6:9, "And let us not grow weary while doing good, for in due season we shall reap if we do not lose heart."

Philippians 4:13, "I can do all things through Christ who strengthens me."

_____
_____
_____
_____

#6. Faith, encouragement, and hope are three important spiritual triplets, so to speak. When we are running low on these, we can make withdrawals from our spiritual bank accounts, so we don't become overdrawn.

Is there someone the Holy Spirit is laying upon your heart to whom you can gift some encouragement?

_____
_____
_____
_____

Quoting Winston Churchill, "Success is not final, failure is not fatal; it is the courage to continue that counts."

"May the God of hope fill you with all joy and peace as you trust in Him, so that you may overflow with hope by the power of the Holy Spirit." (Romans 15:13 NIV)

Sheila Eismann, Prophetic Seer, Blogger, Author & Teacher, publishes her weekly blog posts endeavoring to encourage others through God's word. Her writings include teaching and instructions on how to apply prophetic insights for daily living.

Please subscribe to receive new blog posts on her website at www.sheilaeismann.com. by clicking the "Subscribe" button in the far upper right-hand corner of her Home webpage.

My prayer is that you have been encouraged and challenged as you have worked your way through this prophetic workbook and learned so much more about The Holy Spirit and His Gifts along with the revelatory realms of heaven.

If you have never trusted Christ as your personal Lord and Savior, I sincerely hope that you would consider doing so this very moment. To bring Him into your life, you need to admit your sin and inability to save yourself and ask Jesus Christ to save you. Ephesians 2:8-9 tells us, "For by grace you have been saved through faith, and that not of yourselves; it is the gift of God, not of works, lest anyone should boast."

Jesus has promised to save all who desire to turn from their sins and call on Him in faith. The Bible also instructs us in John 1:12: "But as many as received Him, to them He gave the right to become children of God, even to those who believe in His name:"

Taking a short walk down "The Roman Road to Salvation" is an easy way to ensure that your name is written in The Lamb's Book of Life. Instructions for accepting Jesus Christ as your personal Lord and Savior could not be made easier:

"that if you confess with your mouth the Lord Jesus and believe in your heart that God has raised Him from the dead, you will be saved. For with the heart one believes to righteousness, and with the mouth confession is made to salvation."

Romans 10:9-10

ABOUT THE AUTHOR

I'm an author, blogger, poet, and speaker who has published fifteen (15) books and contributed to three (3) collaborative works. Also, I'm third in my lineage of five female published poets and writers.

During the summer of 2020, I began writing a weekly blog post. "Prophetic Insights For Daily Living" features spiritual teachings, messages, inspiration, words of encouragement, self-reflection, application, and contemplation. My primary emphasis is to encourage others to apply the word of God to their daily lives in a very practical and meaningful way.

While I write in various genres, the west and all things genuinely western are some of my favorite things. Having worked in accountancy, agriculture, the legal field, various administrative capacities, and within the church realm, I pen fiction and non-fiction based upon varied life experiences.

Reading can take us places we've never been before as we learn and discern from the author's voice printed between the covers of a book or appearing on a digital screen. I hope that you will be encouraged, laugh, gain wisdom, and continue to read as much and often as you can.

Serving as one of the original co-founders of ICAN (Idaho Creative Authors' Network), I enjoy speaking at Women's and Writer's Conferences. One of my main endeavors is to enhance the lives of others through education and encouragement. Being a wife, mother, and grandmother, my motto is, "Teamwork makes the dream work!"

Discovery alert: Learn more about me, read & subscribe to my weekly blog posts, and discover my books at www.sheilaeismann.com.

Where to find Sheila Eismann online:

Email: sheila@sheilaeismann.com

Website: www.sheilaeismann.com

Facebook: www.facebook.com/sheila.eismann

Blog: www.sheilaeismann.com

LinkedIn: Sheila Eismann

Etsy: Sheila's and Dan's books are also featured online in Sheila's Etsy shop: www.etsy.com/shop/BooksbySheilaEismann

Sheila invites you to check out her new website **www.sheilaeismann.com** and sign up to receive her blog posts in your email inbox. Please send her an email at **sheila@sheilaeismann.com** to say hello and to let her know what ministered to you the most in this workbook or your favorite blog post. Happy reading and studying!

OTHER BOOKS AVAILABLE FROM AUTHORS SHEILA EISMANN, DAN EISMANN & DESERT SAGE PRESS which can be purchased from: www.sheilaeismann.com or www.amazon.com.

Read and study with **Sheila Eismann,** Prophetic Author, Blogger, Speaker, and Teacher, in Volume 1 of her latest series titled ***Prophetic Insights for Daily Living.*** This **231-page** workbook can be used as a stand-alone devotional, individual Bible Study, or in a group study. Sheila describes various dreams, visions, prophetic words, and teachings she's been given by The Holy Spirit from August 2020 through December 2020 which are designed to help you grow in spiritual knowledge and the operation of The Holy Spirit gifts. Each entry includes questions, contemplation, reflection, or a call to action.

Read and study with **Sheila Eismann,** Prophetic Author, Blogger, Speaker, and Teacher, in Volume 2 of her latest series titled ***Prophetic Insights for Daily Living.*** This **234-page** workbook can be used as a stand-alone devotional, individual Bible Study, or in a group study. Sheila describes various dreams, visions, prophetic words, and teachings she's been given by The Holy Spirit from January 2021 through May 2021 which are designed to help you grow in spiritual knowledge and the operation of The Holy Spirit gifts. Each entry includes questions, contemplation, reflection, or a call to action.

Read and study with **Sheila Eismann,** Prophetic Author, Blogger, Speaker, and Teacher, in Volume 3 of her latest series titled ***Prophetic Insights for Daily Living.*** This **234-page** workbook can be used as a stand-alone devotional, individual Bible Study or in a group study. Sheila describes various dreams, visions, prophetic words, and teachings she's been given by The Holy Spirit from May 2021 through October 2021 which are designed to help you grow in spiritual knowledge and the operation of The Holy Spirit gifts. Each entry includes questions, contemplation, reflection, or a call to action.

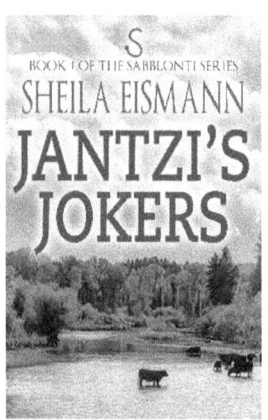

Western Fiction Book One of The Sabblonti Series, ***Jantzi's Jokers***, features Jantzi Belle, the matriarch of the Sabblonti family, who has worked for decades to keep her cattle empire intact. Life takes a drastic turn when she receives a late-night visitor. The brief disappearance of her Last Will and Testament could complicate matters between her daughters, Stormy and Sarita. Stormy and her husband, Chet Castins, are struggling to work through the loss of their three children. Against all odds, drifter Wyn Moreland makes a bold move when he decides that Sarita is his beauty to rescue. The county veterinarian, Dr. Ben Shaw, is also vying for her affections. Will Wyn emerge as the winner? Just before the dawn of the New Year, revelations come forth regarding forgery, cattle rustling, and land exploitation. Will the Sabblonti Empire survive, and more importantly, who will control its reins?

The Sabblonti Saga accelerates in Book Two of the Series, **A Stormy Year**. Riding her high horse after inheriting the family fortune, Stormy Castins is determined to reinvent herself following her husband's accident. Blinded by jealousy, ambition, and naivety, she hires Less and Meg Alotto to oversee her vast high desert mountain domain. While Stormy is away, the cattle herd ends up in disarray.

Amidst the hot dry season, romance is blooming on several fronts despite a major showdown during a mid-summer celebration. The pesky Black Raven continues to wreak havoc at the most inopportune times.

Unable to overcome the vengeance which strikes by way of a mysterious range fire combined with the dire deeds of a cagey couple, the Sabblonti Ranch is in shambles just as Stormy starts to regain her senses. Humility is the prescription needed to open her eyes to realize what's truly important in life. The sparks from a belated holiday Rendevous set Chet and Stormy on their path to recovery.

Desperation explodes when heiress Stormy Sabblonti Castins calculates her dwindling fortune in Book 3 of the Sabblonti Series, **Love the Tie that Binds.** Is she capable of learning the painful lessons of having to rely upon someone and something other than inherited wealth? As her husband, Chet continues to heal from his near-fatal accident, tormenting shadows of The Black Raven lurk in the background.

These high desert hills are alive with blessed babies, enchanting engagements, skillful scavengers, sophisticated scoundrels, rich revelations, timeless treasures, and western weddings.

The Main Sabblonti Ranch house abounds with an unexpected marriage, childrens' voices, and Sir Shelton sporting his silver bell.

In a captivating story of courage, trust, and faithfulness, will Stormy still be tied in knots or find lasting love by the year's end?

Share the joys and sorrows of a mountain community in this swirling saga.

In this collection of true stories titled **Stirrings of The Spirit,** author Sheila Eismann invites you to walk with her family through several valleys en route to some mountain tops as they learned to rely on God in the most harrowing of circumstances.

Have you ever wondered why you were the last one to hear of THE big social event of the year? Well, wonder no longer after reading this e-book titled **Recognize Your Circles**! When volunteering for an organization years ago, author Sheila Eismann was introduced to the concept of "the circles of your life." Since the idea was so beneficial to her, she decided to share it with all of you.

Straight from the Horse's Trough is a humorous read to assist the suburbanite or urbanite who desires to live a healthier lifestyle by growing his or her own food, but is faced with the challenge of a small space in which to do so. This e-book is chock full of how-to steps and includes pictures to remove the guesswork from the project.

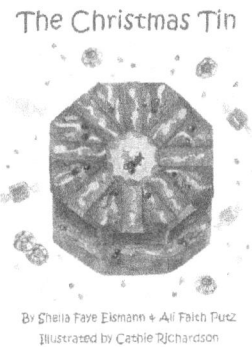

The Christmas Tin is a most delightful read for the young at heart anytime during the year. This endearing book is based upon a true story featuring the older of the two authors when she was a young girl and conveys the timeless message that "love truly is the best gift of all." Children will especially enjoy all of the colorful illustrations contained within this treasure. There's a sugar cookie recipe included in the book and a helpful holiday suggestion for the kiddos to bless someone who's not expecting it at all!

Freedom is Your Destiny! Vietnam Veteran, Dan Eismann, using combat experiences to illustrate spiritual truths, invites you to take a journey with him as he presents a rock-solid strategy for not only fighting your spiritual battles but winning the all-important war. In the midst thereof, the most vital aspect is realizing you can experience freedom and become all that God has destined you to be!

Settle into your special reading spot; grab a cup of tea or your favorite meal. Be stirred as you read and ponder **Poetry Time, Volume One**; allow Sheila's words to encourage and heal.

Everyone can use a little encouragement ~~ a dose of what is beneficial, ethical, and honorable. **Heart to Heart From God's Word** provides this for you. Penned with humor and wisdom, the daily tidbits are paired with Bible verses that convey life-changing principles which are designed for readers of all ages transcending cultures and continents. This devotional will challenge you to grow and fulfill your God-given destiny. It can also double as a prayer journal.

A Woman of Substance is a practical, interactive, and entertaining 12-week Bible study penned to help equip you to fulfill your God-given destiny and impact the culture for Jesus Christ at the same time. It can be used as a stand-alone study or devotional and works well in a group setting, too. It is designed for women ages junior high through adult.

ADDITIONAL NOTES & REFLECTIONS

Sheila Eismann

ADDITIONAL NOTES & REFLECTIONS

ADDITIONAL NOTES & REFLECTIONS

Sheila Eismann

ADDITIONAL NOTES & REFLECTIONS

ADDITIONAL NOTES & REFLECTIONS

Sheila Eismann

ADDITIONAL NOTES & REFLECTIONS

ADDITIONAL NOTES & REFLECTIONS

Sheila Eismann

ADDITIONAL NOTES & REFLECTIONS

ADDITIONAL NOTES & REFLECTIONS

ADDITIONAL NOTES & REFLECTIONS

ADDITIONAL NOTES & REFLECTIONS

ADDITIONAL NOTES & REFLECTIONS

ADDITIONAL NOTES & REFLECTIONS

[i] Keesee, Ruby, Bible Studies for Women: The Gift of the Word of Knowledge (Caldwell, Idaho, 1990), PP. 1-4.

Keesee, Ruby, Bible Studies for Women: The Gift of the Word of Wisdom (Caldwell, Idaho, 1990), PP. 1-2.

[ii] Keesee, Ruby, Bible Studies for Women: The Gift of Discerning of Spirits, (Caldwell, Idaho, 1990), PP. 1-4.

[iii] Jeremiah 23:28.

[iv] AMG Dictionary – Old Testament, word 5030.

[v] Deuteronomy 18:18.

[vi] Jeremiah 20:8.

[vii] Jeremiah 20:9.

[viii] AMG Dictionary – Old Testament, word 2374.

[ix] AMG Dictionary – Old Testament, word 7200.

[x] Jeremiah 1:7, 9, 11, 12.

[xi] 1 Chronicles 29:29–30.

[xii] 2 Samuel 12:1–4.

[xiii] 2 Samuel 12:5.

[xiv] 2 Samuel 11:2–12:9.

[xv] Luke 1:5, 7, 11, 13, 16–17.

[xvi] 2 Chronicles 24:18–19.

[xvii] Acts 11:27–30.

[xviii] Acts 15:32.

[xix] Acts 13:1–3.

[xx] Jeremiah 1:9–10.

[xxi] House, Paul R. (2008) Note to Jeremiah 1:10. L. T. Dennis (Ex. Ed.), ESV Study Bible, English Standard Version. Wheaton, Ill.: Crossway Bibles.

[xxii] 1 Thessalonians 5:20–21.

[xxiii] 1 Corinthians 14:29–32.

[xxiv] Luke 2:36; Acts 2:17; 21:6.

www.ingramcontent.com/pod-product-compliance
Lightning Source LLC
Chambersburg PA
CBHW080637170426
43200CB00015B/2872